FOUL DEEDS & SUSPICIOUS
DEATHS IN BIRMINGHAM

FOUL DEEDS AND SUSPICIOUS DEATHS SERIES

Wharncliffe's *Foul Deeds and Suspicious Deaths* series explores, in detail, crimes of passion, brutal murders and foul misdemeanours from early modern times to the present day. Victorian street crime, mysterious deaths and modern murders tell tales where passion, jealousy and social deprivation brought unexpected violence to those involved. From unexplained death and suicide to murder and manslaughter, the books provide a fascinating insight into the lives of both victims and perpetrators as well as society as a whole.

Other titles in the series

Foul Deeds and Suspicious Deaths in Bolton, Glynis Cooper
ISBN: 1-903425-63-8. £9.99

Foul Deeds and Suspicious Deaths in and around Chesterfield, Geoffrey Sadler
ISBN: 1-903425-30-1. £9.99

Foul Deeds and Suspicious Deaths in & around Durham, Maureen Anderson
ISBN: 1-903425-46-8. £9.99

Foul Deeds and Suspicious Deaths in and around Halifax, Stephen Wade
ISBN: 1-903425-45-X. £9.99

Foul Deeds and Suspicious Deaths in Leeds, David Goodman
ISBN: 1-903425-08-5. £9.99

Foul Deeds and Suspicious Deaths in Nottingham, Kevin Turton
ISBN: 1-903425-35-2. £9.99

Foul Deeds and Suspicious Deaths in and around Rotherham, Kevin Turton
ISBN: 1-903425-27-1. £9.99

Foul Deeds and Suspicious Deaths Around the Tees, Maureen Anderson
ISBN: 1-903425-26-3. £9.99

More Foul Deeds and Suspicious Deaths in Wakefield, Kate Taylor
ISBN: 1-903425-48-4. £9.99

Foul Deeds and Suspicious Deaths in York, Keith Henson
ISBN: 1-903425-33-6. £9.99

Foul Deeds and Suspicious Deaths on the Yorkshire Coast, Alan Whitworth
ISBN: 1-903425-01-8. £9.99

Foul Deeds and Suspicious Deaths in Coventry, David McGrory
ISBN: 1-903425-57-3. £9.99

Foul Deeds and Suspicious Deaths in Manchester, Martin Baggoley
ISBN: 1-903425-65-4. £9.99

Foul Deeds and Suspicious Deaths in Newcastle, Maureen Anderson
ISBN: 1-903425-34-4. £9.99

Foul Deeds and Suspicious Deaths in Oxfordshire, Carl Boardman
ISBN: 1-903425-56-5. £9.99

Foul Deeds and Suspicious Deaths in Pontefract and Castleford, Keith Henson
ISBN: 1-903425-54-9. £9.99

Please contact us via any of the methods below for more information or a catalogue.
WHARNCLIFFE BOOKS
47 Church Street – Barnsley – South Yorkshire – S70 2AS
Tel: 01226 734555 – 734222 Fax: 01226 734438
E-mail: enquiries@pen-and-sword.co.uk – Website: www.wharncliffebooks.co.uk

Foul Deeds & Suspicious Deaths in

BIRMINGHAM

NICK BILLINGHAM

Series Editor
Brian Elliott

Wharncliffe Books

First Published in Great Britain in 2005 by
Wharncliffe Books
an imprint of
Pen and Sword Books Ltd.
47 Church Street
Barnsley
South Yorkshire
S70 2AS

Copyright © Nick Billingham, 2005

ISBN: 1-903425-96-4

Typeset in 11/13pt Plantin by Mac Style Ltd, Scarborough.

Printed and bound in England by
CPI UK.

Pen and Sword Books Ltd incorporates the Imprints of
Pen & Sword Aviation, Pen & Sword Maritime,
Pen & Sword Military, Wharncliffe Books,
Pen & Sword Select, Pen and Sword Military Classics
and Leo Cooper.

For a complete list of Pen & Sword titles please contact
PEN & SWORD BOOKS LIMITED
47 Church Street
Barnsley
South Yorkshire
S70 2BR
England
E-mail: enquiries@pen-and-sword.co.uk
Website: www.pen-and-sword.co.uk

Contents

The Victorian sense of melodrama was based in real life. The Strand magazine

Introduction

Birmingham is the birthplace of quite a few of my ancestors. It has grown from a small market town to become Britain's second city, engulfing smaller villages around it, until it bumped into other towns growing at a similar pace. Today, outsiders may think of Birmingham as being the whole of the West Midlands conurbation, but the locals know that there are still villages and towns with a distinct identity within the region. There are nuances of accent, areas of different trades, mining and its legacy.

Victorian Birmingham was very different to the city of today. The city had grown into a vast sprawl of workshops and cheap housing because of the incredible number of trades, brilliant transport links and incessant hard work of its people. It was, despite popular images of the Industrial Revolution, a

Birmingham's canals saw plenty of suspicious and foul deeds. The author

fairly healthy place to live. Cities like Manchester relied on country folk moving in to replace the workers that died so young that they never had a chance to raise their own families. Birmingham workers managed to raise their children and thus lay the foundations of a strong community. Manchester and its like would have died out without immigration from the countryside, but Birmingham was a city that could sustain and renew itself.

My own Birmingham ancestors turn out to have witnessed or been the victim of some rather dark events. Five generations ago Frederick Billingham, probably from Cradley Heath, travelled to Italy and joined Garibaldi's army in the unification wars there. He returned without seeing a great deal of action and settled down to make jewellery and bash other bits of metal in true Brummie fashion. A generation later Henry James Skinner managed to get himself shot in his pub in Temple Street and another of my great great grandfathers fled from Paris with a price on his head. He settled for a while in Birmingham and founded another metal bashing company that was to make his son wealthy. My grandfather managed to avoid being shot or getting involved in any revolutions, but having joined the Royal Flying Corps in the First World War, managed to crash his plane on its first flight. He survived and eventually married the lady ambulance driver who pulled him from the wreckage. Family history is certainly full of interesting tales.

The research I did for my own ancestors soon turned up a whole realm of stories about other Brummies, often far more dramatic than my own. Victorian Birmingham was a seething mass of people crowded into tiny houses set between workshops and foundries. Guns were unlicensed, poisons available at any corner shop, knives were part of everyone's toolkit and then tempers, inflamed by exhaustion and alcohol, finally snapped. The official history of the city may well portray the diligent hard work, civic pride and phenomenal success, but the city coroner's notebooks reveal the true cost in human terms.

The winners may well write big and official history; but real history is about the lives and experiences of ordinary people.

Only a few relics of Victorian Birmingham still survive. The author

Countless hard working people lived, worked and died without getting a mention, or even any thanks, for the part they played in the creation of Birmingham as the workshop of the world. Hopefully the accounts of some of their more traumatic moments in this book will give the modern world some insight into their lives.

Birmingham seems to have been a surprisingly crime-free city, despite the various gruesome tales in this book. The people needed only a small police force and community pressure ensured that most people behaved in a civilised manner. Of course things did go wrong from time to time, but really evil and malicious characters were very rare indeed. The city was, nevertheless, a regular port of call for the State Executioner.

A century has passed since most of the events in this book. The city has changed physically. Between the Luftwaffe and city planners, huge areas have been transformed from back to back housing to industrial estates. Streets that housed thousands are now simply rows of workshops. Oddly enough the only surviving buildings are often the pubs on the street corners. In part, it is a shame that so much has been destroyed but then who would want to live in such ancient and squalid houses today? The survival of the pubs is a vivid demonstration that the focal points of the community have survived, and that, itself, is something to be celebrated. The huge rows of workshops making anything and everything would swell the hearts of our ancestors with pride. Just ask any local, past or present ... Birmingham can make anything.

Crime has not changed one little bit in the century; there were gangs of youths with odd hairstyles and guns in Victorian Birmingham just as there are now. You are still much more likely to be murdered by your spouse than a stranger, and when it all gets too much, the canals still offer a way to end it all ... and they are much cleaner these days too (though much shallower ...).

The canals appear quite often in this book. I must admit to some bias here, since I have studied and played on the things since I was a lad. Nonetheless, Birmingham has a vast canal network and given the nature of all these dark deeds, it was

The Old Wharf, *a typical Victorian pub, in the heart of the community.* The author

often the private and secluded nature of the canals that caused them to be the scene of an incident. They may not have quite the romantic appeal of Venice, but there's lots of them and they're much more interesting. Without the canals Birmingham would still be a little country market town.

So here follow some of the darker episodes of Birmingham's history. If it all gets too much, please phone the Samaritans rather than throw yourself in the canal, ... it's bad enough getting an old carpet off the propeller.

CHAPTER 1

The Hockley Parricide
1892

PC Shaw quickly cut open the man's collar to find a massive cut in his neck, right through to the carotid artery.

William Workman was about as unpleasant a man as you could wish to meet. His wife, Emily, and two sons, William (21) and George (19), were terrorised by him. Their neighbours in Ventnor Road had become fairly used to the quarrels and rows coming from No 21.

William, aged about forty-five, was a boot and shoemaker by trade, although in September 1892 he decided to try an alternative career as a coin counterfeiter. It was not too difficult for him to find, some Plaster of Paris to make the moulds, some base metal with a low melting point and a few tools. The coins were not up to much by the light of day but you could pass them in a dark and busy pub. William Workman also liked his drink, to excess.

By 29 October he had been kicking his heels around the house when he was not getting drunk and everyone's nerves were on edge. William had been drinking heavily all day. He came home in the evening in a filthy temper and started smashing up the furniture. He then rounded on his wife and threatened to kill them all. His sons William and George managed to calm him down a bit. George went out to try and find a policeman. In this he failed, but half the street heard the noise. Ada Mellows from down the road went into the house to find William pinning his father to the floor, pleading for him to calm down. George Willis from next-door came in and assisted William. The old man simmered down a little and they released him, with the words:

'Father, will you please forgive me for holding you down, I did it to protect my mother.'

'I'll stab you to the heart before I go to bed tonight, and I'll serve her the same,' he replied.

William senior stormed off into the night. He came back at nine, this time brandishing a half brick. He accused his wife of plotting to have him put away, threw the brick through a window and left. Emily followed him out and saw him throw another brick through an upstairs window where her aged father slept.

'I'll smash the old —— tonight' he shouted.

Emily managed to calm him down a little and took him to a pub for a soda water to try and sober him up. It was not a good idea as he then met some men who took him into another pub in Burberry Street. Emily gave up and went home. There she found that her younger son, George, had decided to go and spend the night with friends. She advised son William to go upstairs and keep out of the way when his father returned.

William Workman lay dead on the floor. The Strand Magazine

Emily went out and found her husband in Farm Street. She guided him back to the house. No sooner than they were inside than he started shouting at her,

'You are alone now, the two kids are drunk, I'll show you who is gaffer now, you have no one to take your part now'

With that he bent down and grabbed the heavy fender from the fireplace and raised it to strike her. She wrestled it from his grasp and he shouted that he would smash everything in the house and burn it down. If she fetched forty police he would kill them all.

William's son heard the commotion and rushed down stairs in his trousers and boots.

'Mother we must have help; he means murder tonight.' Emily raced out of the door to get help as father and son wrestled in the hall. She returned with PC Shaw in a few minutes. Her son opened the door, to reveal his father lying in a growing pool of blood between the kitchen and parlour. PC Shaw quickly cut open the man's collar to find a massive cut in his neck, right through to the carotid artery.

PC Thomas arrived soon after and young William explained that his father had pulled his shoemaker's knife on him after Emily had left. They struggled and William pushed his father's arm back. The wickedly sharp knife had been in the old man's hand, and had sliced into his neck by misfortune.

William was arrested for the killing of his father, but as the details of the night's event became clear at the coroner's inquest it was obvious that it was either self-defence or an accident. The coroner returned a verdict of Homicide by Misadventure and William was due to appear before the magistrate the next day. There the police decided to offer no evidence against him. With the cheers of hundreds of his friends he walked away a free man.

CHAPTER 2

Mayhem at Winson Green
1892

Bleeding and battered, Joseph Beasley was lying on the floor, his chest so damaged that the broken ends of his ribs were sticking through his skin.

Our attitudes and responses to mental health issues have changed greatly over the years. In Victorian times a more compassionate way of dealing with lunatics replaced the barbaric methods of earlier generations, but this was not without its dangers. Birmingham had its own asylum at Winson Green, part of a complex of institutions built on newly developed land between the old and new Birmingham canals. The Asylum was state of the art for its time and prided itself on the humane treatment of its inmates.

People found their way into the asylum for a variety of reasons. Senile dementia was one standard reason. It was not

Birmingham Infirmary grew to be able to deal with the many illnesses afflicting the people of the city. John Marks Collection

that common a disease for the simple fact that most people did not live long enough to get it. Joseph Beasley, a street hawker from Deritend, had managed to get to the remarkable age of eighty-three, but through the summer of 1892 his mental state worsened rapidly. He became helpless and losing his memory. His wife did the best that she could but by early December he was in such a state, and she was so exhausted, that he was admitted to Spring Hill Workhouse Infirmary. The staff at the workhouse were unable to deal with dementia and so they sent him over to Winson Green Asylum. There he was placed in Ward 6. This was where new inmates were kept for a week, for evaluation and constant bed rest.

James William Barnes was only fifty-nine when he started to suffer from memory loss. James was a well-known bottle merchant with premises in Banbury Street and a house, 'Champagne Cottage', in Stoney Lane. He was a well-respected member of Birmingham society. Indeed he was a strong man and had been known to step into an affray to help out the police when they were outnumbered. Once he had thrashed a gang of four youths attacking a lone policeman. Ill health finally reduced him to a shell of his former self. His wife nursed him constantly for several months but, on 4 December, he too was admitted to Ward 6 in the Asylum with severe memory loss.

Dementia and memory loss were not the only reasons for admission to the asylum. More severe mental disturbances cropped up from time to time as well. Joseph Allsop was a horse-dealer who had moved to Birmingham from Leeds just before the previous horse fair. He moved into lodgings with his wife at a house owned by Mrs Scott at 127 Suffolk Street. Here the couple lived a quite normal life, although on occasion he was known suddenly to become violent to his wife, and then be filled with remorse and apologies. His horse-trading business seemed to go well. In an era where horses were the prime method of transport, it was a busy sector of the economy, very much akin to car sales today. On a Saturday towards the end of November, one of his deals went awry. During the dispute over a horse he had been beaten and came home with a black eye and battered skull. His behaviour changed over the weekend.

On Monday he started writing dozens of letters; to be precise his wife did the writing as he dictated. There were letters to lawyers and letters to relations. Most of these were incoherent ramblings that made little sense. One theme of the letters to his relatives in Nottingham, his home town, was all to do with a licence that he had once had there for the slaughter of old horses. This was a valuable business opportunity and he seemed to think he would make a fortune from it. At other times he broke down in floods of tears muttering that everyone thought he was cranky but his wife would be all right. Several of the letters were pleas to his relatives to look after her.

His grip on reality loosened through the week. He started thinking that God was inspiring him to do certain things and he started to pray fervently. Three evenings in a row he was thrown out of Day's Concert Hall for his erratic behaviour. By Thursday he was all set to pack his bags and move to Derby to start a new business. His wife, now distraught at his odd ways, was nearing the end of her tether. At four in the morning he woke up the entire household, telling them they must all go with him to the Queen's Hospital to pray for a doctor there.

Birmingham Heath was developed in the early nineteenth century. Along the Dudley Road were built The Asylum, Hospital and Workhouse. John Marks Collection

Saturday morning found him wandering Suffolk Street, hammering on the shutters of the house next door and rambling incoherently. He was still shouting and ranting on at lunchtime when PC Ryan found him. Believing him to be drunk he arrested him. It soon became clear that he was not drunk at all, and the police called Dr Ross Jordan. Jordan certified him to be insane and Allsop was taken to the Asylum that afternoon, apparently quietened because God had told him not to say anything more about Mansfield. He was placed in Ward 6 alongside Beasley and Barnes.

As it was a Saturday, most of the inmates were keenly anticipating their weekly entertainment. This was a performance of Byron's *War to the Knife* by the Warwick House Amateur Dramatic Society. The new admissions had to be kept in their ward but most of the other inmates were in the hall not far from Ward 6. One warder, Mr Willicot, patrolled the cells and wards to look after those who were too sick to attend.

At nine, a series of shouts and screams interrupted the performance. Mr Willicot ran down the empty corridors to Ward 6. He had checked it only ten minutes before and the men had been quiet. Now a scene of mayhem confronted him. Allsop was attacking James Barnes, bashing him about the head with a chamber pot. Bleeding and battered, Joseph Beasley was lying on the floor, his chest so damaged that the broken ends of his ribs were sticking through his skin. Another inmate had crawled under his bed and cowered in mortal terror as the demented attacker wrestled with the warder.

Willicot blew his whistle and several other warders came to his aid. Allsop struggled fiercely, and it took three of them to subdue him. The frail old Beasley had now died of massive injuries to his heart and Joseph Barnes was unconscious for another hour. When he came to, he was able to describe how Allsop suddenly jumped out of bed muttering something about God telling him to avenge himself on the people who had defrauded him, and pounced on the old man in a manic attack.

Rumours of the events soon started to leak out into the city. Embarrassed, the Asylum tried to keep matters quiet, but

The Psychiatric Unit of Dudley Road Hospital was a typically Victorian building. Nowadays its large gardens have been turned into a housing estate and less imposing accommodation built for the patients. The Author

reporters from the *Gazette*, *Post* and *Mail* were soon at the doors. Mrs Barnes was brought in to see her husband. He seemed to rally after the attack, but within a couple of days weakened noticeably, and by the time a week had passed he died, apparently of pneumonia. A post-mortem revealed his skull had been badly fractured. Allsop was sent to Broadmoor for the rest of his days.

CHAPTER 3

The Summer Hill Stabbing
1892
Enraged and fuelled with drink, Costello charged Clark, knocking him to the ground.

I n Victorian times there was very little a woman could do if her husband turned out to be a real thug, apart from run away. Society generally turned a blind eye to domestic violence and many women suffered in silence, unable to bring the force of the law against their abusers. The trouble caused eventually spilt over to the whole neighbourhood.

George Costello and his wife and children lived in a court at the back of Brass Street, near Summer Hill. George was not averse to giving his wife a thrashing when he had drunk a few pints. It was the talk of the street, and she often appeared with bruises and black eyes. Occasionally she sought refuge with the family next door, Mr & Mrs Clark, returning home once the brute had sobered up. Jane Clark did what she could for her friend. Her husband, John, was not a particularly strong man and worked at the delicate task of cutting and making pearl buttons.

By 20 August 1892 matters had become so bad that George Costello threw his wife and two children into the street. Mrs Costello took her children to the Clark's house and pleaded for help. They brought her inside and said she could stay with them until something better turned up.

Saturday 27 August saw George Costello finishing his work as a bird catcher in the afternoon and going out and getting drunk. He was missing his wife and decided he wanted her back. He turned up at the Clark's home in Brass Street at half past nine.

Mrs Costello was out, and George barged into the room shouting that Jane was harbouring her somewhere. Jane swore she was only looking after her friend. Costello turned to John and said he was as bad as his wife. He then pushed Jane so hard she fell into the pantry. John picked up the poker from the fireplace and threatened Costello with some of his own medicine. Costello knocked him down and ran back into the yard swearing and cursing at the top of his voice. Things calmed down in the Clark household and Jane started to get supper ready. To do this she needed to go down the street.

Once in the street she met Costello. He started ranting at her and gave her such a kicking that she fled to her neighbour, Mrs Kimberley. Half fainting with pain she got back home a few minutes later. Costello had run off.

'Oh he's at it again is he?' said John, pulling up his sleeves and picking up the long poker. He went out into the street.

Jane Skidmore, in the bakers in Summer Hill, saw the two of them meet. John had his poker and Costello had something similar in appearance. They fenced with these improvised weapons for a while until John almost managed fetch Costello a blow across the shoulder. Enraged and fuelled with drink, Costello charged Clark, knocking him to the ground. Once down Costello continued to attack him with what was probably a dagger or bayonet.

William Skidmore rushed out to break up the fight, as did John Cheshire. John lay on his back, and quietly said, 'That will do, you have done for me'. Costello turned tail and ran off home.

John Clark was rushed to hospital, bleeding from several deep stab wounds. Sergeant Thomas arrested Costello at his house. He was sobered up by all the adrenalin and realised the dreadful nature of his actions. He wished a thousand times that it was him in hospital instead. It did no good; John Clark was mortally wounded, with internal bleeding and a punctured lung. He gave an account of the events leading up to the fight and, on the following Tuesday, he died. Costello was charged with manslaughter rather than wilful murder on the grounds that Clark had initiated the final fight. Costello escaped the gallows as a result.

It really should not be thought that Birmingham women were all poor little things at the mercy of their husbands, or for that matter that pokers don't make exceedingly effective weapons. Some abused wives fought back …

Some years later, on 11 September 1911, Maria Sofia Woolley finally snapped. Although she had been married to Mark Henry Woolley for many years, and had two grown up children living at their home in Dora Road, Handsworth, recently her husband had started becoming violent towards her. Just the previous week he had punched her about the face.

At nine-thirty on the evening of the 11th, their daughter, Ida Blanche Woolley was upstairs in her bedroom when she heard a disturbance downstairs. She went down to the kitchen to find her father hitting her mother about the head. She had no idea what the quarrel was about, and managed to get between them to stop the fight. Maria went into the sitting room, but Mark followed her in with the intention of hitting her again. Maria picked up the poker and threw it at him.

The poker flew with unerring accuracy and considerable force directly at Mark's head. It struck him just in the corner of his eye, and stuck there. He collapsed unconscious and Ida wrenched the poker out of his eye.

'What have I done?' gasped Maria, 'I wish my hand had dropped off before I took the poker out of the fender.'

It was a bit late; Mark was laid out on the couch, breathing weakly. They bandaged him up and hoped he would recover.

The next morning Inspector Heappey of Handsworth Police arrived. Mark was still unconscious on the couch and he retrieved the bloodstained poker.

'That is the poker, I did it in self defence, I hope he will get better.'

He did not. The blow had smashed the bone at the back of his eye and caused massive lacerations to his brain. He died the next day.

Maria was charged with 'manslaughter under great provocation' and released on bail.

CHAPTER 4

The Aston Axe Murder
1893

In a ghastly shadow play they saw Haynes lift an axe and strike Florence's head ...

Florence Clifford was only seventeen when her mother's dire warnings about her boyfriend came true. Florence had left her mother's home to live with William Haynes and his mother in Waltham Street, Aston. Florence's mother had grave doubts about William. He was ten years older than Florence and had a reputation for being quarrelsome. Mrs Arabella Clifford did not know the half of it. William Haynes had a past. He had started off in the Navy, but when things got a little too dangerous there, he had blown the end of his right index finger off to get out of further service. His hands and arms were covered in tattoos, including one of Florie Walton, his previous girlfriend. His fresh complexion and blue eyes may have helped dispel the rumours of his bad temper; but he was well known to the Birmingham Police as a nasty thug with a record of house breaking. It had not been many months since he was released from prison for beating Florie Walton to a pulp with a heavy hammer.

Around June 1893 Florence went to live with Haynes. Life in the Haynes household certainly failed to live up to her expectations and quarrels and rows, and then beatings and black eyes became her everyday experience. Working at Kynoch's in Lodge Road, Florence rarely had time to see her family. Eventually she did get a chance to visit her mother, and after a little prompting poured out her tale of abuse. She was at her wit's end because she was now pregnant with Haynes' child, and it seems this had brought out the very worst in the man, the beatings had become intolerable. Arabella realised that Florence really had to leave Haynes and move back home on 19 September.

Haynes seems to have been unmoved by the news that Florence was moving back to her mothers. He shrugged his shoulders and told them to come round to his house the next day to collect Florence's clothes. That day he finished work at lunchtime and went out and got very drunk. He got home in time for dinner in a right state, according to his mother, but went upstairs to sleep it off. Florence and her mother duly arrived at the house in the evening. Darkness had descended and Florence went into the kitchen whilst her mother stayed in the yard. Haynes' mother came out of the house and the two of them talked for a while. A terrifying scream interrupted them. The blind on the kitchen window revealed the silhouettes of Florence and William inside. In a ghastly shadow play they saw Haynes lift an axe and strike Florence's head, the grisly sound clearly audible in the quiet night. They rushed inside to behold a scene that would scar them for life. Florence was lying on the floor, Haynes standing above her hacking at her head with a wood axe. Haynes flung the axe at Mrs Clifford and fled from the house, up Waltham Street and disappeared into the night.

Florence was barely conscious, and bleeding heavily. Mrs Haynes rushed to the pub across the road to get help whilst Arabella cradled her daughter's battered head in her arms. Their little pet dog, a fox terrier, licked Florence's face as though to try and help. She had several massive gashes in her skull and her one ear had been sliced off. They managed to get her to hospital, but Florence slipped into a coma despite surgery. Haynes fled the city.

Five days later Florence died and the hunt was on for a murderer. The police extended their search for Haynes further afield. Florence and her mother had not known that Haynes was already married to a woman in Wellingborough and that he had worked at a brewery in Northampton. The police set up a constant watch on the woman's house, hoping that he would turn up there. In the city, the detectives' department were getting constant information about Haynes' whereabouts, but they all seemed to be dead ends. It did transpire that Haynes' real name was Harris. The trail seemed to go cold when suddenly Haynes walked into the police station in Northampton and gave himself up. Inspector Cusack took the train to Northampton and arrested him. On the return journey Haynes admitted that he had done the dreadful deed, not that there was much doubt in anyone's mind about that. He seemed to think that it was all the fault of the girl's meddling mother.

The court case was quite short. The jury heard a rather half-hearted plea from the defence that Haynes had been incapable through drink and so it should be a verdict of manslaughter. The judge did not agree with that one little bit, it was clearly wilful murder. The jury did not even bother to retire to consider their verdict; it was unanimously guilty. With that the Judge put on his black cap to deliver the death sentence. As he started to speak, Haynes burst out.

'I wish I could have cut up her mother and all - I would have chopped her into mincemeat, made sausage of her.'

The rest of his words were drowned out in the uproar. The judge restored order and tried to continue with the sentence but Haynes interrupted again, 'I am ready for it'. He continued muttering even as he was dragged down to the cells, saying 'I wish I could have chopped her mother up, then I would have been satisfied'. He was hanged a few days later, a cold and callous murderer, unrepentant to the bitter end.

CHAPTER 5

The Sad Demise of Ada Burden
1892
... there was such a huge social stigma for unmarried mothers.

Domestic service was a key element of Victorian society. Almost extinct today, then virtually every middle class household had a retinue of servants. For the most part the system worked well, providing valuable employment on one part, and luxury and status on the other. However, it did not always go smoothly.

In August 1892 Ada Elizabeth Burden started her job as domestic servant at 68 Summer Hill Road. It was the well-to-do household of Mr W B Parker, the manager of the Patent Borax Company. Mr Parker and his wife had two sons, Edgar Charles and William Bailey. There was a day housekeeper, Mary Ann, and an errand boy, Harry Ward. Both Ada and Edgar were seventeen, whilst William was a year older. Ada had a boyfriend when she started, William Whittacker, who used to send her love letters, but behaved like a perfect gentleman towards her. Within a month of starting her new job, she broke off their relationship.

Ada got on well with her new employers and all too well with Edgar. By

A perfectly respectable family. The Strand Magazine

November he had got her into bed. This was not an entirely unheard of occurrence, and just once in a while such relationships ended in wedding bells. More often than not the servant girl would be used until appeal waned and would be chucked out. Generally, Victorian society frowned on such liaisons and there, is reason to suppose that, if Edgar's father found out, he would be furious. Such activities in his household would lower his status in the community. Edgar was found a job at a discrete distance, in Coventry and, in April, had to leave the family home. His

An indecent proposal. The Strand Magazine

brother, William, was studying Chemistry at the Midland Institute, and being such a credit to his family, was allowed to build his own laboratory at the back of the house. In neat cupboards were ranged rows of bottles of reagents, acids and poisons.

Ada was now pregnant, but told no one. The full style of Victorian dresses helped to conceal her growing bump, but as the summer wore on Ada realised something had to be organised. She had been writing letters to Edgar, but was not getting the kind of answers that she needed. Edgar pointedly refused to answer the important letter telling him about the expected baby. Edgar was coming home about once a month, and, when there in June, she told him she would come to stay in Coventry during her holiday.

She went to stay at the beginning of August but Edgar was not going to help her with her approaching confinement. Even whilst she stayed with him in Coventry, she still had to cook his breakfasts, still just a servant girl and not the long hoped for partner of a successful young businessman. Ada returned to Summer Hill not really sure what to do. She spoke with her mother but did not reveal that she was pregnant. She was in a precarious position since there was such a huge social stigma for unmarried mothers. Ada sought advice from a medium, paying to have her fortune told. It seems that this provided no clue as to her best course in life. Indeed it would have been a very brief consultation.

Edgar returned home for the weekend of 11 August. His parents were away and his uncle, William Jackson, was staying in the house. No doubt he and Ada had many long conversations over the weekend, but things were not resolved. The baby was due in a matter of weeks now. Ada would end up on the social scrap heap if he made no provision for her. Edgar had had his fun, and saw no pressing reason why he should do anything more. On Monday morning she brought him his breakfast and apparently seemed happy enough when he left to catch the train back to Coventry. Harry Ward went off to do his errands at eight-thirty.

Ada certainly was not happy. At her wits end she wandered around the empty house until she found her way into William's laboratory. There, clearly marked with skull and crossbones, was a bottle of potassium cyanide. She took it up to her room and drank it.

Mary Ann arrived at nine-thirty, and let herself in through the front door, the back being locked, which seemed unusual. The house was silent. Upstairs she found Ada lying on the floor in front of her dressing table, dead as a doornail. Luckily Mary Ann did not try applying the kiss of life, or she

'You are the father.' Strand Magazine

would have died too. Young Harry arrived and was quickly sent off to fetch the doctor.

The inquest revealed the sad facts concerning the suicide of Ada. Her callous treatment by Edgar attracted only mild criticism by the coroner, but in 1892 such behaviour was not uncommon. He was labelled a bit of a cad, and the affair forgotten.

CHAPTER 6

The Sparkhill Scandal
1894
*The man squeezed through the gap in the hedge
and they realised that there were two bodies there.*

amily life has always had its dark side; relationships that change over the years can strain to breaking point. One case seems to have caught the public imagination both in its thoroughly unpleasant nature and in its aftermath, casting Birmingham society into a vivid and critical light.

The Birch family seemed a perfectly normal household in 1894. Edward and Selina Birch lived at 59 Upper Highgate Street. They had several children of their own and also Caroline, a child that Selina had borne before they were married. Caroline was now eighteen and clearly growing up to be an attractive woman. Sometime during the summer of 1894, Edwards feelings towards her changed from those of a normal step father to something far more sinister and manipulative. It seems that he may have caught Caroline with a young man, possibly Albert who worked at the same engineering works with her. Perhaps this event made him realise that she was no longer a child but a desirable young woman. Birch, who was thirty-five, embarked upon a scheme to entrap and seduce Caroline.

In August 1894, a letter arrived for Caroline. She opened it and read:

Dear Calley, I did not see you as arranged on Sunday. I hear you was at Moseley on Saturday night with another young man. I don't know how your clothes was but it took me 2 hours to clean mine next morning. I seen you on the doorstep on Monday night. I hope you will meet me on Sunday night 7:30 At the corner of Balsall Heath Road and Moseley Road. With best love and kisses, yours affectionately, Don't disappoint.

Caroline burst into tears, swearing that there was no such young man and it was all a joke or a hoax. An untruth. Selina had a nasty suspicion that her husband had had the letter written for him. She was somewhat concerned that something was amiss ever since Edward had started taking Caroline to music halls and the theatre.

Furiously protesting her innocence, Caroline insisted that there was no young man, and to prove it she would take him to the meeting place on Sunday night to prove the matter. Selina must have had grave doubts about the whole business. She secretly followed them, and watched as they waited ten minutes on the street corner. The two of them then walked off down Sherbourne Road, although Selina followed them no further. In the following

Caroline receives a strange letter.
Strand Magazine

weeks, Edward kept a close watch over Caroline, escorting her to and from work and to her night school.

Whatever Selina's suspicions, nothing untoward happened until the Christmas period. The festive season seemed to bring out the very worst in the increasingly jealous Edward. He had seen her in the company of a young man outside the factory where she worked. He accused her of 'keeping company' with him, called her a liar when she denied it and generally called her for everything. She tried to run away from him, but he caught her and hit her with a stick. Crying and bleeding from the mouth she returned home.

The next Sunday Lily, her stepsister, overheard Edward and Caroline talking in the house. He was trying to persuade her

Mosley Road, Birmingham. Was this where Caroline Birch met her secret lover, or was she being victimised by her stepfather? John Marks Collection

to go 'somewhere particular' with him. Caroline complained that she was too tired, so Edward arranged the tryst for Monday evening. Caroline protested that she had school that night and half an hour would not be long enough. Quite what they were arranging Lily could not hear. Suspicions about their behaviour were now extending well beyond the family circle and into the neighbourhood.

Heavy snow blanketed the city and its surrounding fields through January. Edward went to work on Monday 7 January 1895 and told the foreman, Joseph Dagmore, that he had to attend court for not sending his children to school. He tried to borrow money from his workmates at Lowe's to pay the fine. Edward returned at about three, with red eyes and seemed to have been drinking. The red eyes may have been caused by the accident he had just seen. A barrel had fallen of off a wagon and burst open. 'What stuff is it?' he asked, 'Something that people poison themselves with.... Car ... something.' 'Carbolic Acid' suggested Joseph, 'Yes that's it.'

At five when it was time to leave, Edward took off his jersey and said to his fellow iron plate worker, James Myatt, 'I'll leave this here, it will do for you to work in.' James really did not know what he meant.

Edward had been home to Upper Highgate Street just before returning to work at three. He told his wife that he would be going out to a supper that evening so she need not worry if he came home late. At seven Caroline left the house to go to evening classes at Shebourne Road School.

At nine o'clock Louisa Marshall and a gentleman were walking along Springfield Road when they heard a groaning sound coming from the field next to Mr Stanbury's house. The man squeezed through the gap in the hedge to see what two dark shapes were in the snow. Louisa came through the hedge and they realised that there were two bodies there. They managed to get a little whisky into the man's mouth, but the girl was clearly dead; there was a two-inch gash in her throat. Quickly they raised the alarm. Arthur Lewis, a brick maker who lived nearby at Malvern Villa, came over to help, but apart

Springfield Road, Sparkhill. The route of their last walk. Edward Birch was carrying both poison and a knife as he took Caroline along this road. John Marks Collection

The Mermaid Hotel. *The Worcester coroner had to perform a hasty autopsy by the flickering light of a candle in a shed at the back of this pub.* John Marks Collection

from trying a little more whisky on the man, there was little anyone could do.

An ambulance arrived and took the dying Edward Birch to the Queens Hospital. Caroline, already dead was conveyed to an outhouse of the *Mermaid Hotel* nearby. Edward died within fifteen minutes of arriving at the hospital.

The question soon arose. What on earth had happened? Why had it happened?

Caroline's body was laid out for autopsy by the Worcestershire coroner at the back of the *Mermaid.* The stable must have been a macabre sight, lit only by a couple of candles the table was too short and was threatening to collapse. It was soon evident that there were no signs of a struggle. She had drunk a large amount of carbolic acid and was probably already dead from shock when someone had stabbed her in the throat with a sharp knife. Caroline was not a virgin, but she was not pregnant either. The coroner decided that she must have drunk the acid willingly as there was none spilt around her. It did not take long to work out who had stabbed her.

Back at the Queens Hospital the Birmingham coroner had better conditions to work with, Edward Birch had died from drinking carbolic acid too.

The next day a policeman found a carving knife in the snow at the scene, to go with the bottle of acid and cup that had been found the previous night. Edward's pockets revealed three letters and other sundry items. Selina Birch was beside herself with grief, and was heading for a complete nervous collapse when she found that the cup used to drink the poison was the very one that Edward had given her for her 32nd birthday, lettered 'A Present from Birmingham'.

The motives behind the murder and suicide were partly revealed by the letters, but not to any great degree of satisfaction. Edward seemed to try to absolve himself and blame everyone else. The question as to why Caroline had willingly drunk a ferocious poison remained clouded in mystery.

The first letter was in a bloodstained envelope. Inside was:

Written Nov 8th 1894, this is to show I will not be bested. I worned her 12 months ago. She don in 5th May 1894 what she ourt not to. I court her _____ and forgive hir & the mother thought it was work that made hir bad then & so she deceived me agin and when I get in drink plays on my mind and I make a beast of myself. I've taken hir out & to places of amusement and then she will be after the men & in September last I give hir lef to go to Sunday school & church if she be in by nine and then she goes of with to fellers In the rain until after ten at night round the Moseley fields covered with muck and paint when she gets home she sed that she had been at a girls house in Vincen Street the name of Florry Savvers who had been with hir and told the same lie I have tried to fined out who they was but cannot she defies me She is not my own child and this is the reason when I tell hir about it the mother takes hir part and incurers hir in it. So this is the end of it. I ham no scholler so make the best of it.
Edward Birch

The second letter was addressed to Edward's father and was heavily censored for the press. In essence Edward stated that he had caught Caroline in flagrante with a man, and since she was not his own blood, he had the right to do the same. He then seems to indicate that he has got her in trouble, presumably he meant pregnant, and ' this is the way out of it'.

The third letter was addressed to Mr Walker, the owner of the engineering firm where Caroline worked:

> *Dear Sir, you myte find that fooll Albet the tool maker something better to do than trying to get roung a girl by telling them that press work was not fitting ...' He goes on about how jumped up Albert is for a while and concludes ' Please send heir mother what she as coming to 59 Upper Highgate Street. As you will not see her alive again.*

It was not long before a verdict of murder and suicide was reached. The murderer was Edward Birch and he was dead. There the sorry tale should have ended but for the morbid curiosity of the city.

The jurors felt so sorry for Mrs Birch that they gave her their one shilling fee for attendance and several citizens sent donations to her via the newspapers. Joseph Locke started up a fund to help her.

After the inquest the two bodies were removed to Joseph Adams' Mortuary in Sparkhill. The following Sunday night they were put on display, at a penny per viewing. Posters advertising the gruesome spectacle appeared all over the district. Crowds descended on the undertakers to see what was going on.

The affair exploded into the papers the next day. 'Disgusted' of Edgbaston started a virulent attack on the undertaker and all those who went to see the bodies. The pages of the *Daily Gazette* resounded to barrages of complaints and accusations of desecration. Several thousand people paid their penny but Mrs Birch, who had initially supported the idea, changed her mind. Joseph Adams decided that the money raised was to be given to Mrs Birch. He conducted the funeral and cremation free of charge. The scandal rumbled on for a few more days before normal life resumed.

CHAPTER 7

The Shooting of Henry James Skinner

1895

The Bulldog-pattern bullet, quite capable of felling an ox, buried itself in the wainscoting. Skinner turned back towards the noise and the next shot caught him in the side of the chest as he turned.

Thursday, 5 December 1895 started off as any normal day for Henry James Skinner. He was the well-respected manager of the *Bodega*, a public house in Temple Street. It was the haunt of actors and athletes,

After the murder the Bodega *was refurbished and renamed the* Trocadero. *Luckily the façade has remained unchanged since then.* The Author

enjoying a good reputation at the heart of the city. Henry had become the manager in 1889 after a long career as boxing and fencing instructor. His many former pupils formed the clientele, joined by the actors that worked with his daughter Helen at the Olde Royal Theatre. It was a busy, orderly pub.

The pub itself was a small community; David Andrews was the head bar manager and two brothers, Herbert Edward Allen and Arthur John Allen, were the barmen who had both worked there since leaving school; whilst down in the cellars Henry Duller looked after the barrels. Herbert and Arthur also worked as jobbing builders, although Herbert had been injured in a fall from a tree the previous summer, suffering a broken jaw and strange mood swings ever since. The cellar-man, Henry, felt that he had become a different man since the fall.

On Tuesday night Henry Skinner had found some bottles left uncorked behind the bar. He pointed this out to Arthur and some sharp words were exchanged. Henry slammed his hand down on the counter for emphasis; unfortunately Arthur's hand was in the way. Hurt, Arthur hit Henry in the face. Henry walked around the bar, but Arthur's brother, Herbert, fearing that his brother was about to get a thrashing from one of the city's leading boxing teachers, grabbed hold of Henry's coat to restrain him. Henry managed to grab Herbert's wrists and several customers and the head barman held him

Shot after a trivial argument, Henry James Skinner was the great great grandfather of the author. You never know what you'll find in family history research. Birmingham Gazette

Henry Skinner as a young man in the Guards Regiment. Authors Collection

down. The bar calmed down slightly, but Henry Skinner sacked both brothers on the spot and escorted then off the premises. They were told to come back the next day for their wages.

Tempers had cooled by Wednesday morning. Arthur went to the *Bodega* to get his wages and to apologise. Henry Skinner paid him and offered to provide references to help him get a new job. Arthur asked for his old job back, but Henry was standing by his decision. However, Herbert was becoming increasingly distressed.

At twenty-three-years-old he was just starting his life; he married his sweetheart the month before and the couple were sharing a house with his brother. The loss of both their jobs seemed catastrophic. He turned up at the *Bodega* about half an hour after Arthur, but seemed so excited that David Andrews refused to let him see Skinner, and turned him out of the bar, telling him to return the next day. Within half an hour his other brother, Charles, found him drunk in Suffolk Street.

Herbert and Charles went to the *Wheatsheaf* at the corner of Severn Street. They stood talking in the yard when Herbert pulled a revolver out of his pocket. 'This is meant for Skinner,' he said. Charles told him to throw it away and Herbert threw it to the ground. The gun fired as it hit the floor. Herbert cried that life was just not worth living, but Charles paid little attention to that. Ever since the fall, he had been complaining of a pain behind his eye and often threatened to kill himself.

Charles walked him back to his house in Upper Gough Street and put him to bed. Whilst Herbert slept, Charles searched his room and found a dozen or so cartridges, but no trace of the gun. He dropped the cartridges into a drain on his way home. Herbert was no better when Arthur returned home that evening, still threatening to shoot himself. Arthur had been to the *Bodega* that evening and David Andrews suggested that things could yet be patched up and their jobs saved.

Thursday morning got off to a bad start. At eight-forty-five Arthur met Henry outside the *Bodega* as he collected his letters from the post box. He apologised again and asked for his job back. Henry refused and

Possibly suffering brain damage from an accident, Herbert's mood swings had tragic consequences. Birmingham Gazette

said Arthur could take out a summons for assault if he wanted. Arthur left disappointed and angry. Herbert arrived at the *Bodega* at nine o' clock with the rest of the staff and went to the office for his pay. Henry Skinner gave him his wages without a word. Herbert left without any comment. During the morning Arthur decided that, with no hope of reconciliation, he might as well take out the summons for assault. He might just get some compensation. After visiting a lawyer he met up with his brother. They walked back down Temple Street to the *Bodega*.

Henry Skinner was standing on the doorstep, getting ready for his usual morning walk about the city. He called Herbert over and said, 'It is just according to what Art does whether you come back or not.' Herbert shrugged and went into the bar to collect his bag of building tools. Unaware that Herbert might get his job back, Arthur told Henry Skinner about the summons and walked away disappointed. Herbert collected his tool bag from the end of the bar and asked David for a couple of brandies. He seemed worryingly tense and excited. David said he would have to ask Mr Skinner, who was just coming in through the door. He assented but David replied 'I think not.' Henry Skinner said it was not a good idea, 'Arthur has taken out a summons against me for assault'. Henry turned away from Herbert and took a couple of steps towards the bar.

Herbert called 'Mr Skinner ...' and pulled out the revolver, firing towards Skinner. The Bulldog-pattern bullet, quite capable of felling an ox, buried itself in the wainscoting. Skinner turned back towards the noise and the next shot caught him in the side of the chest as he turned. He collapsed to the floor with a sigh. David leapt over the bar and grappled Herbert to the ground, ripping the gun from his grasp. Outside, PC Owen had heard the first shot and was already running towards the pub by the second one. He entered to find several customers pinning Herbert to the floor, whilst others sat stock still, paralysed with the shock of the sudden horror. Henry lay dead. The bullet had penetrated his heart. Herbert, guilty of wilful murder, was given a life sentence.

The Vyse Street Outrage
1896

*He looked a bit closer and was horrified to realise
it was the battered body of a little girl.*

There are some murders that seem pretty run of the mill affairs. When Duncan Jones's reign of bullying drunken terror was brought to a conclusive end by two boatmen and a hefty wooden tiller handle, no one was that bothered. The boatmen walked free. There was one murder that was so foul, so hideous, that the law seems incapable of providing a suitable punishment. It is a problem that still perplexes society today. The Victorian solution may not be appropriate today, but it was very effective for its time. There was no repeat offence.

On 10 March 1896, little May Lewis, who was just ten years old, left her home in Smith Street to go back to school after lunch. She may have met someone on the walk to Summer Lane Board School because at the end of classes she took a different route home. Her school friend Florence Poyner said that May cut across the boys playground towards Brearley Street, saying that it was quicker. Florence had never known her go home that way before. May was used to walking home alone and knew the district well. Her little sister usually walked home alone before May.

Henry Hodcetts later saw May with a man in Hockley Street. Henry was working at 89 Vyse Street, and saw the man opening the double doors that led into the back of 93 Vyse Street. Henry noticed this because he knew that the house was empty. He did not think it was important until a couple of days later. It was the last time May was seen alive.

Number 93 Vyse Street was not exactly empty. It was being renovated prior to being rented out. The caretaker and his family were staying in the upstairs rooms and the ground floor

Tell me there's a heaven, tell me that it's true, *Chris Rea. The Strand Magazine*

was in the process of redecoration. Edward Lewis of Ryland Road was alone in the house, painting the dining room, at about five o'clock when he heard someone let himself in and walk across the hall. Edward thought nothing of it since the caretakers were in and out all the time. About an hour later he tidied up and went home. Apart from the footsteps he heard nothing unusual.

Edward returned to work at six-fifty the next morning. The police had taken control of the house. Half an hour before, John Williams had been walking along Vyse Street when he saw something odd in the corner between the bay window and wall of number 93. He looked a bit closer and was horrified to realise it was the battered body of a little girl. He called the police from Hockley Hill. Sergeant James Thomas found May Lewis, the child that everyone had been searching for since the previous evening. She had massive head injuries, her clothes were torn about and saturated with water. James Thomas rushed off to get a doctor. They returned a few minutes later. She had been dead for some twelve hours, the doctor concluded. The Sergeant saw a movement inside the house. He banged on the door.

Most of the caretaker's family were there. Lizzie Taylor, the seventeen-year old daughter, opened the door; the policeman asked where her father was, instructed her to send him down, and to go upstairs and stay there. James Thomas did not wait long, he met John Taylor on the landing. He told Lizzie, John's

Vyse Street, the scene of an utterly despicable murder. Inside the house bloodstained the floors and walls. The Author

wife Maria and the youngest son, Ernest to stay upstairs. John was to come downstairs with him.

In the hall James Thomas opened the dining room door. There was a large stain of blood on the floor.

'What's that?' he demanded

'I washed the blood off.'

'What blood?'

'I washed the blood off the floor. I did not want her to see it.'

James Thomas was deeply suspicious. He asked who else lived in the house and John Taylor reluctantly admitted that he had an older son who did not really live with them but came round last night.

'I went out and stopped until nearly one o' clock because my son was the worse for drink.'

Frank Taylor was nowhere to be found.

James Thomas stopped his questions and called for more police to help. A thorough search of the house and an autopsy revealed the terrible fate of May Lewis. The little girl had been violently outraged, the Victorian term for rape, her assailant had then knelt on her so hard that her liver had ruptured, and beaten her head with a brick repeatedly. The house was steeped in blood. The assault appeared to have taken place in the bedroom that the younger son used. The bed was soaked with water and blood, there was blood on the sink and a brick in the fireplace was also covered in it, with the child's hair matted onto it. There was a bloodstained towel in the kitchen and traces of it on almost every floor of the house. Someone had tried to clear it up, but simply managed to spread it even further. Who that person was needed to be discovered urgently, before the maniac could harm another child.

John and Maria were immediately arrested for being concerned with the incident. Lizzie gave a clear account of the previous evening from her perspective. She had returned home from her job as a clerk at about eight; and her father let her into the house. Her brother Frank was asleep on the sofa,

Vyse Street. The abused body of May Lewis was carelessly dumped just below this window. The Author

but woke up when she was rummaging in the bureau for something. He dozed off again straight away and Lizzie went to meet her mother, who had been out cleaning all day, at the corner of Great Hampton Street. Her mother did not turn up so after ten minutes she returned home. A short while later her mother came back and Lizzie went out again to pay her club money. She returned at about ten past ten. Her father had gone out and Frank was combing his hair, getting ready to leave. Her mother sent her out on another errand to Hockley Street. She got back in a few minutes to meet Frank in the hall. Her father followed her inside, but her mother immediately sent her out again, this time to get some beer for her father.

She returned with the beer in time to see Frank being given a half penny by his mother, and walking off into the night. He was drunk. Inside the dark house Lizzie was puzzled. Looking for a candlestick she found a child's hat and cloak in Ernest's bedroom and there was blood all over the bed. She took the cloak and hat down to her parents. She knew something was very wrong.

Maria told John to go and have a look round the place. When he was gone she said to Lizzie, 'I know he would not do anything to a little one when he is sober, but there is no knowing what he would do to anyone when he is drunk.'

Her father was gone for some while, searching the house by the light of an oil lamp. Lizzie and her mother were too frightened to go and see what was taking him so long. Ernest returned home and that night he had to sleep in Lizzie's room, not knowing his own bed was drenched with the blood of the little girl. Lizzie lay awake most of the night. As daylight filtered through the windows she saw the bloodstains across the floors, and downstairs they were everywhere. It was with relief that she opened the door to Sergeant James Thomas and let some fresh air into the nightmare she had endured.

The police were anxious to talk to Frank Taylor. He had spent sometime drinking in a pub with Thomas Gumley about lunchtime on the 10th. This pub, *The Saint Matthais Tavern*, was on the route May Lewis would have taken to return home. Gumley left Frank Taylor near there at about 4:30. No one then saw Frank until Henry Hodcetts briefly saw him entering the Vyse Street house with a little girl. The next person to see him was his father, who found him standing by the door at seven-fifteen. By now he was very drunk. They were alone together until Maria came home at nine. She noticed blood on his shirt cuff, but Frank told her he had cut his finger.

He had left the house around ten-thirty. Nothing is known of his movements until Wednesday night. It seems that in his drunken, crazed state of mind he decided to kill himself by drowning. Joseph Cousin and his mate were bringing a boat along the old canal near Lodge Road when they saw someone in the water. Frank Taylor had discovered that the drawback of trying to drown oneself in the canal is that it is pretty shallow. He was standing on the bottom with his head sticking out of the water. He did not have the courage to fully immerse himself. They threw him a rope and he dragged himself out, and walked away without a word. Shortly afterwards he walked into Dudley Road police station and was charged with the outrage and murder of May Lewis.

The case came to court on 30 July 1896. By today's standards the evidence against Taylor was circumstantial and weak; the doctors could not even identify the blood on the

Winson Green Gaol. Taylor was held here until moved to Warwick, to be hanged. Although the public were excluded from the gallows, a black flag was hoisted over the gatehouse when the hanging was completed. John Marks Collection

doorstep as human, let alone May Lewis's. None the less the jury and the press were convinced that Frank Taylor was indeed guilty of this horrible crime. The Judge, Justice Wills, had no hesitation in sentencing Taylor to death.

In Victorian England there was no hanging around on death row for years. Frank Taylor was executed on 18 August. The Sheriff and prison authorities decided that they would exclude the press from the execution much to their annoyance. Public execution had been halted in 1868, but the press jealously guarded their right to observe and report that justice had been done. Some of the journalists thought something might be being done very differently on this occasion.

A huge crowd gathered outside Warwick Gaol, including the whole family of May Lewis. At eight o'clock the black flag was raised, and a huge cheer resounded. Frank Taylor had been hanged. It was not long before rumours started to circulate that his execution was not quite as clean as it could have been. Not that anyone was particularly concerned about that.

Taylor himself had to be subject of an inquest to ascertain that he had been legally and properly executed. The usual practice was to drop the prisoner a specific distance and let the rope snap his neck, providing instant death. There was a table of weights and distances that the hangman used to make sure that this happened reliably. Mr Billington, the hangman, added an extra two feet to the drop in this case, ostensibly to make sure of a quick death. In fact the result seems to have been quite the reverse. Perhaps the knot was in the wrong place or the calculations incorrect, but the result was that Frank Taylor was strangled, the rope cutting deeply into his throat.

Public opinion was outraged; not because of Frank Taylor's suffering, the general feeling was that it was no more than he deserved, but because the press had not been allowed to witness and report his fate.

CHAPTER 9

The Killing of PC Snipe
1896

A rain of small stones had been thrown ... but now someone threw a brick with deadly accuracy.

The life of a policeman in Birmingham was every bit as precarious as anyone else's. Indeed sometimes far more so. There were not a huge number of them and for the most part civil order was maintained by general consent. Ordinary people wanting to live in a world free of crime ensured that rogue elements were swiftly brought to justice. Social pressure ensured that for much of the city, life was orderly and the police were respected. However, some parts of the city were closer to a constant state of anarchy and revolution. It was here that the police were treading a fine line just to survive. The niceties of polite social behaviour tended to get lost on people who were struggling to avoid starvation, living in over-crowded squalor and watching their children die needlessly. It took very little to trigger a riot.

Police Constable George Snipe and his colleague, PC Frederick Mead, were on patrol in New John Street on a quiet summer's Sunday evening, when they noticed a gang of young men in a particularly boisterous mood. They followed them into Guest Street and on into Bridge Street West. One man was getting out of hand and they were forced to arrest him for using obscene language. Mr Coleraine was unimpressed and put up a fierce struggle. The gang he was with followed, and was joined by more people

PC Snipe was knocked down simply because he bore a passing resemblance to another policeman. Birmingham Gazette

roused by the commotion. Coleraine managed to wrestle PC Snipe to the ground when they were just outside the *Star* beer-house. By now the crowd had grown to several hundred, few of whom were sympathetic to the police. Those in the pub swelled the mob. Coleraine was subdued, and the policemen started to drag him towards the nearby Bridge Street station.

A rain of small stones had been thrown at the pair, but now someone threw a brick with deadly accuracy. It struck PC Snipe on the left temple, crushing his helmet and knocking him unconscious. PC Mead frantically blew his whistle for assistance, and several more responsible citizens tried to assist the fallen PC Snipe. Mead decided that with PC Snipe being tended by these people, he would get Coleraine into the Station.

Police from the station joined their colleagues attracted by the whistle, and at ten-fifteen were starting to regain control of the milling throng, now in excess of 700. The Good Samaritans who tried to help PC Snipe had been elbowed away, although John Miller pushed his way through and found the poor policeman still unconscious and being trampled underfoot in the crush. He managed to help one of the policemen drag PC Snipe to safety. PC Burnall, on the periphery of the melee in Wells Street was handed a strange present. It was the very brick, grabbed as a souvenir by the eleven year old, Henry Gibson. Also in Wells Street, a young man by the name of James Franklin, handed PC John Parry Snipe's helmet. The mob was eventually dispersed by about ten-thirty, and PC Snipe was rushed to the General Hospital. It was to no avail, as he had sustained a massive head injury from the brick and numerous bruises from peoples' feet. He died at two-thirty the next morning.

As the dust settled on the streets, the search for whoever had thrown the brick started. There were hundreds of witnesses, but few sympathetic to the police and little help was forthcoming. After making such progress as they could, James Franklin was arrested and charged with the murder. It was a very weak case, relying on the fact that it was Franklin that had handed over Snipe's helmet. James Franklin was also a well liked lad whose friends rallied around him and in his defence identified the real culprit, George 'Cloggy' Williams.

Cloggy Williams had been drinking in a pub that evening, nursing a grudge against the policeman whose evidence had got him sent to gaol for a couple of months. PC Holdsworth was very similar in build to PC Snipe and Cloggy, thinking it was he, joined the throng outside the *Star*. It was the work of a moment for him to pick up a brick from the gutter and heft it with devastating accuracy at PC Snipe. He turned up his collar and got away from the scene as soon as he heard the scream.

'Cloggy' Williams was eventually arrested when his money and luck ran out. Birmingham Gazette

The next morning, with all the newspapers full of the details, he realised that not only had he killed a policeman, but also that he was the wrong one. He had to get away. With a man known only as 'Chicken' Jones, he walked to Stafford. On the way they saw a paper with the details and Cloggy remarked to Jones that he wished he had never thrown the stone, not for a thousand pounds. Cloggy effectively disappeared.

As soon as the case against Franklin collapsed, posters appeared for the arrest of George 'Cloggy' Williams. At first in Birmingham and gradually all across the country his face adorned police station notice boards. Meanwhile, Cloggy seems to have gone to Bolton and tried to get work in an iron foundry but since he had no 'Society' card he failed. The same happened in Newcastle. He turned southwards, tramping the lanes until he reached Gloucester. There he managed to find work as a cattle drover, walking alongside the vast herds of cattle that regularly walked the byways of England towards the vast appetite of London. The pay was miserable and the work gruelling. He eventually returned to the place he called home.

On 29 January 1898, after six months as a fugitive, Cloggy Williams was standing on a street corner shortly after midnight. He was close to his mother's house in Clements

Street and no doubt hoping for a warm welcome. It was not to be, the somewhat insomniac Sergeant Moss was taking a short cut home when he spotted a familiar outline in the dark. He went straight up to Cloggy and arrested him.

At his trial there was a heated argument about whether he was guilty of wilful murder or manslaughter. The crux of the matter was that if he had intended to kill PC Snipe by chucking a brick at his head, then it was wilful murder and he would face the gallows, if he had intended to merely injure or annoy PC Holdsworth, but killed Snipe by accident, then the charge should be manslaughter. The jury decided it was manslaughter and Cloggy Williams was sentenced to prison for the rest of his natural life. Given the conditions of prisons in those days, it was not that long.

CHAPTER 10

Poverty and Child Funerals
1898, 1901
The sad array of wreaths and mourning cards grew through the day.

The lot of the working people of Birmingham was not a particularly happy one. Poverty was endemic and led to a high infant mortality rate. Stillbirths and neo-natal deaths were rife in the cramped, damp tenements. The close proximity of the thousands of factories belching out smoke and poisons, piles of horse muck in the gutters, all combined to create slums in which only the strongest survived.

Another mouth to feed in a household barely able to cope was a problem; but when a baby died the additional cost of a burial could be catastrophic. It was occasionally possible to

The source of considerable civic pride, the neat Victorian Cemeteries of the city were too expensive for many poorer people. John Marks Collection

Dudley Road as it was when Inspector Goldrick made his ghastly discoveries.
John Marks Collection

save money by using informal contacts. Many a respectable Birmingham lady was buried with a tiny corpse tucked into her coffin unbeknown to her family, a sort of post-mortem fostering.

It was not always so tidy. As with the rest of Birmingham industry, if you knew someone who worked in a trade you could strike a deal. In this case it really was not a good idea.

WH Scott, jnr, was an undertaker at 281 Dudley Road, Winson Green. He was, needless to say, a very busy man. In September 1898 he noticed that some of his shrouds, coffin boards and handles had gone missing. Suspicion fell on one of his workers, William Woodhead. Mr Scott contacted the police and Detective Sergeant Goldrick and PC Durkett were dispatched to search Woodhead's home at 275 Dudley Road, on the corner of Heath Green Road, on Monday 5 September.

Goldrick soon found some the stolen goods, but this was only the start of grisly series of discoveries. Pervading the house was a foul smell and Goldrick decided to investigate the garret, where the odour was strongest. Here he found more of the stolen coffin parts, and next to them were some stillborn babies. Further into the attic he found three boxes from which a powerful smell of putrefaction came. Woodhead admitted that it might take seven to nine days before a child was buried, but then denied any knowledge of the bodies, or the seven death certificates that the detective found. Woodhead was instantly arrested and the boxes conveyed to Kenyon Street Mortuary. Another box was found hidden behind the ash cans in the yard.

Strangely enough, William Woodhead was innocent of any crime; his arrest was as much to do with securing his safety from the growing crowd of grieving parents. The law of the land stated that any child who had breathed before death must have its death registered, a stillborn needed no paperwork at all. Bizarrely, even though there was a ten shilling fine for not registering a death; there were no laws at all governing the subsequent burial and storing up the sad little bodies was entirely legal. There was even a small-scale trade of body parts from undertakers for dissection. Most undertakers buried

Dudley Road in 1908. John Marks Collection

infants in small collective graves in churchyards. William Woodhead was simply gathering a sufficiently large collection to make this economically viable. The parents of these children did not see things in quite the same light.

The coroner started to attempt to identify the bodies. By working with the death certificates he managed to identify most of them. They were in very poor condition and this was long before anything as sophisticated as DNA analysis. Typical of the individual tragedies was that of Mrs Richards.

Mrs Richards had been recently widowed and life then dealt her a second blow when her child of only 4 weeks died in April. She was already in debt before running up a bill of £4 with the doctor. There was simply no way that she could afford a funeral, and so she carried the body to the undertakers. There she found that the place was closed, but there was sign on the door directing out of hours visitors to call at Mr Woodhead's house. There Mr Woodhead said that he would arrange for the child to be buried at Smethwick cemetery for the sum of 9 shillings. She paid him the money and left the body with him.

Mrs Richards was unlucky. Had she called when Mr Scott was there and arranged the matter properly, he would have only charged her 5 shillings, and got the job done promptly. Evidence like this ensured that Woodhead continued to be remanded in custody. The rumours had circulated around the city and he would have been torn limb from limb if released. Other undertakers took note of the public sentiment. In a gruesome clearing of stock, a couple of days afterwards a couple of badly decomposed female infants were found in the canal nearby.

Mr Scott was absolved of any blame in this sorry tale. He was found to run his business scrupulously. The same cannot be said of one of his rivals.

'Arthur Knowles', undertakers of 193 Newtown Row, was run by Arthur's widow, Emma. She hadn't learnt anything from the public humiliation of William Woodhead. Through 1900 and into May 1901 she was offering cut-price burials of infants for only 2 shillings. Considering the church charged 2/6 for an infant burial, someone probably smelt a rat.

Someone certainly smelt something because on 28 May 1901, in a midnight raid, Detective Inspector Davies and PC Moran discovered an even more horrific hoard in the cellar. Through the dark hours the remains of no less than 29 bodies of newly born children were removed to the sanctuary of the mortuary. Some of them had been in there for over a year. The mess was so indescribable that at first they thought they had 31 bodies.

Next day dawned with a huge crowd around the doors. There a sad array of wreathes and mourning cards grew through the day. The shop remained closed from that day on. Emma Knowles was charged with killing all those children for whom there was no correct paperwork. The law was still in such a lax state that for most of the poor little children there was no way of identifying them, let alone knowing whether they had been still born or an infant death. The charges were dropped. It seems that when Arthur Knowles died in 1897 his wife carried on the business, but simply pocketed the cash for infant burials and dumped the bodies in the cellar. She had committed no crime according to the law of the land, although she did decide to move out of the city on her release.

It was to take changes in the law and the building of the city's crematorium in 1903 to put an end to such horrific scandals and to treat the dead children of the poor with the dignity due to every child of the city.

CHAPTER 11

The Latimer Street Murder
1898
A ghastly sight was waiting for them.

Mary Ann Aliban was something of an eccentric old lady aged about 59 or 60. Her father had been a successful shopkeeper who gradually built up a large property portfolio of seven houses in Latimer Street. He died and left this to his wife and in due course she died, in 1883, and left it to their daughter Mary Ann. This allowed Mary to live comfortably off the rents of six of the houses, and live in 60 Latimer Street. She never married, and was rather nervous, not to say even paranoid, about being robbed. This became so severe that in 1888 she was confined to an asylum for fifteen weeks. She returned to normality and Latimer Street only marginally better and gradually became a local eccentric. Everywhere she went she carried two bags, a black handbag and an old carpetbag, reputed to be full of her entire savings, in cash. She even took them with her when she went into the backyard. Sometimes she would get the kids of the neighbourhood to carry the carpetbag for her, and give them three-pence for their effort. The bag was very heavy. If she had to go out for a long time she even paid them to sit on her doorstep so that no one could even think of getting into the house. Needless to say the house was locked and barred, with iron grates on the windows and shutters across the old shop window at the front.

Generally considered harmlessly batty by her tenants, Mary Ann had reached the age of fifty-nine by the time the rumours of her wealth finally reached the wrong ears. She had a predictable routine, each night at about eleven, she popped over to the *Barley Mow* to get her nightcap of half a pint of strong ale that she brought back to the house before locking it all up like a bank vault. It was to be her undoing.

Miss Aliban surprised. The Strand Magazine

Mrs Hewlitt, Mary Ann's tenant and neighbour realised something was wrong on the morning of 20 October 1898. The front door was slightly open, just by an inch, but that was enough to raise her concern. Together with PC Joseph Waters she crept into the house, mostly empty and covered in dust, up the stairs and into the old lady's bedroom. A ghastly sight was waiting for them.

Mary Ann Aliban had been tied to the bed, her right wrist to the headboard, her left to the foot, a handkerchief forced into her mouth and a piece of linen tied tightly around her neck. She was definitely dead. The linen, when unwrapped, turned out to be a blue and white neckerchief. Her false teeth and handkerchief had choked her.

The bedroom had been ransacked, and the old carpetbag she carried was missing. The black handbag was on the floor and Mary Ann's large chest was open and its contents strewn about. The rest of the house seemed fairly empty apart from some footprints in the dust of the cellar. The hunt was on for a couple of murderous burglars.

Caroline Reece lived directly across the road at No 115. She had seen a couple of men leave the house early that morning and walk away quickly towards Irving Street. She described them as both dirty and as Lower Class. She managed to give the police a fairly accurate description of the men she saw.

At the nearby corner shop a man of very similar description bought some cigarettes with coins that were all old and discoloured, a rather odd occurrence that stuck in the mind of the shop assistant. The description was circulated to the newspapers straight away.

At about ten the same morning a man took lodgings in Paradise Street, West Bromwich. He told John Horton, the landlord, that he was tired and had come from Birmingham. He ordered ham and eggs for breakfast but was so nervous, pacing up and down, that he never ate them. He kept enquiring about when the papers came out and let slip that he was in trouble. Eventually the papers arrived in the afternoon and he bought one before retiring to bed. Curious, John Horton read the paper with interest. The description of one of the men sought in regard to the Latimer Street Murder was uncannily like that of his new lodger. He called the police.

PC Wilson arrived and asked the man calling himself Frank Jones to accompany him to the station. The man gathered up his few belongings and went along. He explained the handful of loose change bound up in an old hankie, 15 shillings and 3 pence, as the change from a sovereign that he had found on the pavement in Dudley Road. The coins were all old and discoloured.

In West Bromwich Police station, the dishevelled man was identified as Claude Felix Mumby. He said he had gone to hide because he was frightened of being identified as the man

seen in Latimer Street, and then admitted to being in Latimer Street, but seeing two men answering the description talking to a policeman at one in the morning. The next morning news of his arrest was in the papers and strangely enough his own brothers came forward to supply further evidence against him. They had all lived at 115, where Mrs Reece now lived, and had all known the old lady by sight. John Mumby had even carried her bags once and recalled a conversation with

Claude Felix Mumby was such an obnoxious coward that even his own brothers gave evidence against him. Birmingham Gazette

Claude about getting into the house and grabbing her cash. Charles Mumby, another brother mentioned that Claude had said if he got the money he would hide it until later. Charles also mentioned seeing his brother, in the company of another man who wore a blue and white neckerchief just like the one found around Miss Aliban's neck.

It was the description of the neckerchief that was to provide the next arrest. The master of Erdington Workhouse recalled that Mumby and another man stayed there the night before the murder, and that the other man had a neckerchief of a similar colour and pattern. The police started to watch the workhouses in the area closely. Their vigilance was rewarded on the 28 October when a detective of the Salford force recognised a man from the description, and arrested the 22-year-old George Webb at Salford Workhouse. He was conveyed to Birmingham and charged with the murder.

Both men were in very poor condition when they were arrested, dressed in not much more than rags and half starved. The regular meals they got in the cells visibly improved their condition and made them somewhat more talkative. Mumby spilt the story first. He said that he had met George, whose real name turned out to be James Twitty, in Erdington Workhouse, and together they had entered the house whilst the old lady had gone out to get her beer. They managed to get in through the coal grating, even though the police had discounted this as a means of entry to the house. They hid in the coal cellar until all was quiet and, taking off their boots, crept upstairs. Mumby said that George wanted to do the old lady in, but he said not to. The noise of their conversation woke her up and she started to scream. They tied her up and George pushed his handkerchief into her mouth to shut her up. They rifled through her belongings and took what they could find before getting out of the house.

James Twitty drifted around the workhouses and streets of Birmingham until he fell in with Mumby's plan to rob Miss Aliban. Birmingham Gazette

The case came to court on 15 December 1898. There was plenty of evidence to show that the two had caused the death of the old lady, but little to show that they had intentionally killed her. There was no evidence at all as to the whereabouts of the carpetbag, supposed to be full of cash. The police had found about £100 around the house in old tins and pots. The two accused certainly had not found it. As things stood, intended or not, Mumby and Twitty had caused the death of Mary Ann Aliban and were sentenced to death. The jury had returned their verdict of guilty with an additional plea that the judge should be merciful as they felt it was not a premeditated killing. The judge had no such option unless there was an appeal. Some months later the appeal did decide that the killing was manslaughter rather than wilful murder and the pair had their sentences reduced to life imprisonment. The state of Victorian prisons may have made them wish they had never appealed.

CHAPTER 12

The Peakies
1898

Gloating, Harper then carried out the prescribed gang punishment for girls ...

Gangs of youths have always had their distinct fashions and codes of conduct. It was as true in Victorian Birmingham as it is today. They tended to be engaged in petty crime and fighting amongst each other. Little rituals bound them into a community of sorts and anyone who transgressed their unspoken rules was punished. Such is the timeless nature of young men finding their way into greater society that we can see just the same rituals and behaviour today. Some of it is harmless, some definitely not.

The Victorian 'Peaky' was the lad about town. Bell-bottom trousers, a flashy neckerchief, army style hob nailed boots polished to perfection, and of course a distinctive hair cut. This could be an oiled peak at the front, or a donkey style fringe, depending on which gang the lad was in. An attitude that you could break rocks on was essential too. It all sounds horribly familiar. The attitude also embraced the idea that girlfriends were personal property to be treated like slaves. The girls could not dump their boyfriends without dire consequences.

James Harper, an eighteen-year-old lad from The Grove, Hospital Street, had plenty of attitude. He was an obnoxious thug into the bargain. He was somewhat more handsome than the usual spotty adolescent, having a clear fresh complexion and fair hair. Perhaps it was this that attracted Emily Pimm, although it could have been that he was marginally better off than her; she lived in one of the courts off the back of Hospital Street with her father and sister. The two of them had been walking out together through the summer of 1898.

The trouble started in September when Emily decided to end their relationship and walk out with Charlie Jones instead. This was not in the Peaky code at all, girls just did not do that sort of thing. It was the boys that did all the dumping. James Harper was losing his credibility and he was not happy about it. He started to threaten and intimidate Emily.

Emily was fairly terrified to go out of the house. She knew that the Peaky Code called for some pretty violent retribution, but sooner or later she would have to go out. Her father Frederick was completely ignorant of all this and asked her to go out to fetch him a jug of beer on 1 November. She bumped into Harper in the yard at the back of Hospital Street.

It was the chance Harper had been waiting for. He punched and kicked her, but she managed to retaliate, belting him over the head with the beer jug so hard it cut his scalp open. Harper ran off with blood pouring down his face. Quite what all his mates said about this is unknown, but being thoroughly battered by a slip of a girl must have made him the laughing stock of the whole gang. Harper was not laughing at all; he was just infuriated.

Emily was now virtually a prisoner in her own house, too frightened to venture outside without her friends. Nevertheless on Friday 11 November she decided to go out with Minnie Spalding and another friend, Charlotte. They walked as far as Summer Lane and stopped there to talk to Minnie's friend Joe Jones. Harper spotted them and came running up.

Emily's friends Minnie and Charlotte dragged her home after the first attack. **The** Strand Magazine

Harper was berserk with fury, completely ignoring all the people in the street he smashed his fist into Emily's face, knocking her to the pavement. He then kicked her head with his heavy army boots. Minnie Spalding protested and he turned and punched her. Emily managed to struggle to her feet and run for it. Harper chased her and punched her to the ground again. Emily's head hit the kerbstone and she was knocked out. Gloating, Harper then carried out the prescribed gang punishment for girls: he stamped his foot down hard on her face three times.

The other people in the street, appalled by the sudden ferocity of his attack started to shout out. 'You've killed her'! Harper ran away.

Minnie and Charlotte helped Emily to her feet, she was barely conscious so they half carried, half dragged her back to her house. She was bleeding from the ears and nose. After a while she seemed to recover, so the three of them went to a pub to calm their nerves. Emily continued to bleed from the ears so they decided to get her home again. After a short while she slumped into a stupor and they had to carry her the rest of the way home. Minnie and Charlotte propped her up in a chair, wished her Good Night and left. Emily's father Frederick tended her through the night. She was vomiting and in agony from the battering.

Saturday morning saw no improvement in her condition. Frederick insisted that she went to the General Hospital, but she was even more afraid to go out now. Eventually her friend Emily Bayliss turned up and promised to go with her on the understanding that she would scream loudly if there was any sign of Harper. They got to the hospital without incident. There the doctor prescribed some powders and pills, but without the advantages of modern X rays, there was not much more he could do. Emily did not help herself because she tried to cover up the cause of her injuries for fear that he would laugh at her. She told the doctor that she had slipped and hit her head on the fender at home.

Returning from the hospital they walked straight into Harper once more. He asked her to go for a walk with him that night, but she said she was feeling too sick. He expressed some regret for the previous night and Emily said she would see him the next night.

'You should not have thrown the jug, if you don't come I shall give you some more the first time I meet you.'

Emily clung on her friend as though she was going to faint. She threatened to have Harper locked up but he just laughed,

'I don't care, if I'm out by Christmas.'

Harpers mood suddenly swung. He grabbed her by the hair and punched her in the face once again. As she doubled up in pain he smashed his knee into her stomach and then ran off.

Emily was dragged home in agony for the second time in two days. She lapsed into unconsciousness on the Saturday night and on Sunday she died of a cerebral haemorrhage. Her skull had been smashed in two places. Harper was arrested and charged with manslaughter, and eventually imprisoned. He remained cocky and defiant all through the trial, but no doubt had that attitude thoroughly kicked out of him in Winson Green Gaol.

CHAPTER 13

The Tragic Consequences of Poverty
1912

Horrified, he put the dreadfully wounded body upstairs, and tried to clean up some of the splattered blood.

Before the introduction of the welfare state, life could be very perilous indeed. There was the workhouse, but many people feared that more than death itself. Work was generally short in the spring of 1912, and coal miners' strike made things even more difficult. For the thousands of workers employed in the city, times became extremely hard.

The neighbours helped Thomas Killoran as much as they could. The Strand Magazine

Thomas Killoran was a blacksmith's striker, but in April the shortage of coal became acute and work that had been scare for months dried up altogether. Thomas had done the best he could since his wife died in the previous summer, but it was not easy finding food for his four children. The pressure simply piled up. The winter was hard and the family had moved into one of the ghastly back to backs, No 20, at the back of 185 Ledsam Street. As March progressed the coal finally ran out and Thomas had no work. Through the last week of March what food he had went to the children, he had to do without. His neighbours, Mrs Lucy Smith and Mrs Daniels helped where they could. Mrs Smith used to look after the children while he was working and Mrs Daniels occasionally gave them some food. They both knew the terrible difficulties he was facing and respected the way that he still managed to look after the children as well as he did.

On Sunday 8 April Mrs Daniels gave them three pints of milk. It was a meagre Sunday lunch, but slightly better than nothing. Mrs Smith popped round to warm it up for the children. Thomas Killoran had told her the day before that he simply did not know where the rent money was going to come from. Mrs Smith went home and after lunch Thomas sent his eldest daughter, Mary, aged just seven out on an errand. While she was gone Thomas Killoran finally buckled and broke under the crushing poverty.

Blinded by an intense black depression, he determined to put an end to all their misery. He gathered up his little two-year-old son William, and took him into the kitchen. There he picked up a hammer and started to hit him on the head with it. After four blows he suddenly realised what he was doing. Horrified he put the dreadfully wounded baby upstairs and tried to clean up some of the splattered blood.

Mary returned from her errand just as Thomas, reeling from the enormity of his actions decided he must give himself up to the police. They met just outside the back door. Mary could see the blood on the pantry floor and on her father's hands. He told her, 'Don't go in there, come along with me.' Out in the street in he said, 'Go and tell Mrs Smith to come and do what she can with the little lad.'

A distraught waif turned up on Mrs Smith's doorstep, saying 'Will you come and see to Billy? Dad and Billy have fallen downstairs. He has hurt Billy but he has not hurt himself.' Lucy followed the poor girl back to the house. There she found baby Billy lying on the bedroom floor, his head surrounded by a pool of blood. Lucy shouted for help and Mrs Daniels came running. There was no sign of Thomas.

Mrs Daniels took a look in the bedroom and around the house. The two women managed to get Mr Joseph Weston to take the child to the hospital whilst they remained to care for the other children. Mrs Daniels found the hammer still in the sink, in a bloody pool of water. There was more blood on the floor and a trail up the stairs to the bedroom. William was admitted to Queens Hospital, but despite their care, he died at eight- that evening.

Thomas Killoran walked into the lock-up and spoke to PC Holland. He wanted to give himself up.

'I intended to kill all four of my children, but after the first my heart failed me.'

On the way to the cells he added, 'What could a man do? There is nothing but starvation.'

Thomas Killoran was charged with wilful murder, but was spared the gallows, as he was clearly (at least temporarily) insane.

Thomas Killoran was by no means unique in his response to grinding poverty. A few years later another father was pushed to the brink and beyond by despair.

Robert Speerli was a tailor by trade, and moved to Birmingham from Switzerland. Life had not been good to him in his forty years. His wife had borne him one girl before becoming an invalid. That was eight years ago, and in the early autumn of 1914 she was taken back into the city infirmary. Worse still for Speerli, the outbreak of the Great War meant that he was vilified and shunned because of his apparent Germanic origins. The bigots were not fussy about distinguishing between German and Swiss; Speerli could no longer get work.

Through the autumn and into the winter Robert and his beloved daughter, Mabel, struggled to get by in a set of rooms in Henley Street, Sparkbrook. He had to sell virtually all the furniture to keep the food on the table, and by January he was reaching the end of his tether. It was now that Mabel started to get poorly. Once again neighbours helped out where they could, especially Mrs Punter next door. On January 3rd they spent the evening with her, returning to their cold empty rooms around midnight.

During Monday, Robert Speerli decided he could cope no longer. He started to write his farewell letters;

To Mrs Punter,

Just a few lines to thank you for all the kindness you have bestowed on Mabel and I … things would not have come to this end if people did not interfere with my affairs. Cannot write any more as my head is so bad.

He had turned on the gas tap and the deadly town gas was gradually filling the room. Then he started a letter to his brother-in-law John Lloyd:

I did not think we should last for so long. Recently I have written and gone after a good number of positions but without results. My nationality is against me in several instances. And now we have come to our end. Please pay the money I have borrowed for my insurance and bury me anyhow.

His last letter was to the City Coroner.

The insidious coal gas gradually suffocated the little girl, but there were enough draughts to keep Robert Speerli alive. The hours passed and he realised he would have to find another route out of his vale of tears.

At Haunch Lane, Yardley Wood a man by the name of Thomas Dent found him beside a nightwatchman's fire, not far from the canal. He was completely soaked. 'I've been in the canal' he explained. Dent called the police.

It was a broken and silent man who stood trial for the wilful murder of Mabel Speerli. He barely raised an eyebrow as the jury retired to consider their verdict. Not a word passed his lips as he was sentenced to death and he did not even seemed relieved when the jury strongly and emphatically recommended mercy because of his insanity. He was to spend the rest of his days in an asylum.

CHAPTER 14

The Death of Jane Nash
1900
The Quiet Woman.

Jane Nash was known in the area as The Quiet Woman. She lived in a furnished apartment at No 13 Park Street with her husband William. She had a reputation for being an industrious worker, spending hours putting hooks and pins onto cards, a typical home worker in the city. Whilst Jane was a very sober lady, William was rather too fond of his drink and it tended to make him violent.

Jane had a secret. Although everyone in Park Street referred to the couple as Mr & Mrs Nash, Jane had married Joseph Nash of Smethwick in 1888. William's surname was Harrison. She had disappeared from Smethwick in 1898 and now in April 1900, had completely lost contact with her husband. Nevertheless, she treasured the one reminder of her former life, keeping her marriage certificate close to her heart all the time.

Jane and William moved into Park Street at the start of March. From the outset, Jane became a respected member of the little community and William became despised for his drunken habits and quarrelsome nature. Half the street heard rows almost every morning before William went off to work as a bricklayer. Jane talked with the other women in the street when he was away at work, but once he returned the shouting and occasional beatings would start again. Jane complained to Sarah Ward, who lived in another apartment at No 13, that she just did not know what to do to please him. Jane was not in the best of health, suffering from pain in the neck and head. As March drew to a close she confided to Sarah that she had been to the Queen's Hospital and been diagnosed as consumptive. In the days before anti-biotics this was virtually a death sentence. It was a disease that carried off thousands, usually

The site of Jane Nash's home is now just a car park. Much of the southern half of the city has been extensively altered in the last century. The Author

those living in poor housing and with a bad diet. If Jane had hoped that her partner would be sympathetic to her plight she was in for a rude shock.

William went berserk on the Saturday night. He grabbed the paraffin lamp and threatened to smash it over Jane. Paraffin lamps have a tendency to explode when broken, it was a vicious and callous way to treat someone who needed all the support she could find. William spent most of the weekend drunk. When he returned from work on Monday night he was in the worst temper Jane had ever seen him. She was so terrified that she fled the house and was taken in by her neighbour, Mrs Green. Luckily Mrs Green ran a lodging house, and so had a spare bed for Jane to sleep in.

William Harrison was lurking outside the door the next morning. Jane had to go out, and walking down Park Street, he caught up with her by the railway bridge.

'You ———, where have you been all night?'

He struck her head hard with his lunch bag, twice. Jane collapsed to the ground.

William Harrison, a callous brute who cared nothing that his loving wife was dying of consumption.
Birmingham Gazette

Frank Butler, the potman at the *Black Horse*, rushed to her aid, trying to lift her up.

'Leave her alone, let the —— die.' There were other witnesses, and William took to his heels.

PC Cato and PC Evans were close by and chased William all the way back to his apartment where he had locked himself in. PC Evans had a simple latchkey that soon opened the door and they arrested him on a charge of assault.

Back by the railway bridge Frank Butler again tried to lift up the unconscious Jane, but she quietly died in his arms.

William Harrison protested his innocence all the way to the station. His lunch bag contained nothing more lethal than a piece of bread and meat. He was, nevertheless, remanded in custody on a charge of manslaughter. Jane had died because the rough treatment was simply too much for her frail and weakened frame. William Harrison was sentenced to a period of imprisonment even though he had not actually intended murder.

CHAPTER 15

The Hagley Road Tragedy: the Sad Death of Emma Freeman
1900
Emma's body was thin, dirty and lice-ridden, her skin taught over her bones.

Life in Edwardian Birmingham was divided into sharply marked social classes. If you were born into the right class, life could be comfortable, if not it could be a nightmare. Illegitimate children were especially vulnerable to exploitation and cruelty, trapped into a cycle of poverty and distress that seemed to offer only one route of escape.

The unequal lives and everyday cruelty of the system was thrown into the light when Emma Freeman was found dead on the conservatory roof of her employer's house. Falling from her bedroom window, she was so emaciated that she never even broke the glass.

Emma was fifteen years old and worked as maid in the household of Florence Louisa Lewis at 109 Hagley Road. Emma was called Mary by the rules of the house. Miss Lewis was a spinster who kept a substantial household for a single woman. Fred Parker was the boot boy and Daisy Lewis was the head of the staff. Miss Lewis occasionally took in lodgers and seemed to get through quite a few servants. John Goodman, another lad, had only just left and Amy Brittain and Kate Burr left in the previous year.

Emma's little broken body was taken away for post-mortem. Mary Meredith found the girl was clad in a thin cotton dress that was in rags, a thin chemise made from an old nightshirt, an old pair of men's socks and a piece of torn and filthy blanket around her shoulders. It was hardly suitable clothing for January 1900. Emma's body was thin, dirty and lice-ridden, her skin taught over her bones. The big question was

Daily Argus.

TUESDAY, APRIL 10, 1900.

EDGBASTON SERVANT'S MYSTERIOUS DEATH.

THE CHARGE AGAINST MISS LEWIS

THE DEFENDANT MISSING.

A WARRANT GRANTED.

This morning, at the Victoria Courts, Birmingham, before Messrs Williams and Phillips, Mr Philip Baker mentioned the case of Florence Louisa Lewis, late of Hagley-road, who was summoned, at the instance of the National Society for the Prevention of Cruelty

MISS LEWIS.

, Children, for neglecting to provide proper clothing and food and ill-treating her servant, Emma Freeman. He said that the case had been adjourned in the hope that the defendant would attend, but she was not present. Her solicitor was, however, present, and he understood from him that he did not expect she would come.

Mr Walthall (for Miss Lewis) said he did not think the summons had come to her knowledge, as she went away before it was served.

Mr Barrsdale pointed out that the case was adjourned on the understanding that if she did not appear the warrant would issue.

Mr Williams: The warrant will issue.

There is a statement abroad that Miss Lewis sailed to America last Friday. Mr Clarke Hall, barrister-at-law, an authority on offences against children and author of a standard text book on cruelty to children, will be briefed to appear for the prosecution should the warrant against Miss Lewis be executed.

HISTORY OF THE CASE.

The girl Emma Freeman, aged 19, was on the morning of January 25th last found lying dead on the top of a conservatory at the house, having either fallen or thrown herself out of her bedroom window. At the adjourned inquest, on February 9th, allegations were made that her mistress had failed to provide the girl with sufficient food and clothing. As evidence of her neglect, May

whether Emma had been driven to suicide by jumping from her bedroom window, or slipped whilst trying to escape a life of deprivation and cruelty, or had she been pushed? Mr Bradley, the city coroner opened an inquest.

The facts started to emerge as the initial inquest was reported in the papers. Witnesses came forward and those with something to hide started to plan. The story of Emma's short life became apparent as Mr John Odling of Barnardo's Homes sought to assure the public that although Emma had been in their care, she had been released to a relative and not sold into domestic slavery by the institution. Emma had been into the home in February 1896 at the application of her aunt, Mrs Freeman of Clent, Stourbridge. Emma's father was presumed dead, her mother emigrated to Canada, and she had been brought up by her grandparents until they died and she was passed over to her uncle Joseph. Soon enough his wife died and she was bundled off to her aunt Mrs Pardoe at Belbroughton. She was not too keen on the idea and placed Emma in the care of

Florence Louisa Lewis fled from justice at the last moment, selling up all her furniture just before the detectives arrived. Bimingham Argus

Barnardo's. A couple of months later Mr H Pardoe insisted that she should be released back to their care. An enquiry showed that he did have the means to support her and Barnardo's had little choice but to comply. The next thing they heard of Emma was the report of her death.

Sarah Pardoe said that she answered an advertisement for 'a young girl of about 15'. Miss Lewis promised to feed, clothe and train Emma, although she would not pay her, just provide a little pocket money. Emma was stout and in good health when she left Mrs Pardoe.

A couple of days after the first enquiries began, Fred Parker apparently found a suicide note written by Emma:

Fred, if you or anybody should find this bit of paper, give it to Miss Daisy. I want her to ask my dear mistress to forgive me for what I am going to do. There is only myself to blame. What will the mistress think of me when she hears it. I told her she didn't know I had been turned about before I came here. I love miss — —, I hope Alice will forgive me, Goodbye, Mary Freeman.

It was pretty obvious that the note was not in Emma's handwriting when it was compared to a couple of letters she

had sent to her aunt. It was not the only deeply suspicious occurrence, details of life in the Hagley Road household began emerge and by the time the inquest sat again an even darker picture was apparent.

Robert Nash McCrate was an insurance manager who occasionally lodged at the house. He had often complained to Miss Daisy that the girls in the house seemed weakly, poorly nurtured and apparently unfit for their work.

Locked in the cellar. The Strand Magazine

One Sunday morning a couple of years ago he heard screams and yells. It so alarmed him that he went downstairs and rang the bell. Miss Daisy appeared and said nothing was the matter, but Robert insisted that Fred should be brought up to him. Miss Daisy refused at first but Robert really was worried and eventually she brought Fred. He was sobbing and clearly very upset, but would say nothing in front of the woman. When Robert managed to speak to him alone. Fred said he had been thrashed for being rude to Miss Daisy. Robert threatened to report the matter to the police if it happened again.

Fred seemed to be on the receiving end of plenty of trouble. The staff at the house next door were aware things were not quite right. They had heard him being beaten for asking for his breakfast, at lunchtime, and once the coachman, William, met Fred in the coachyard . He had hardly any clothes on and said he had been locked in the cellar for a week with just bread and water, all for stealing a bit of jam. William asked why he hadn't shouted for help, but Fred shrugged and said he did not want another bucket of water chucked over him.

Just before Christmas, Edith and Rose had heard the sounds of a girl being beaten and crying. Someone shouted 'Now Mary , remember, never let me hear you complain about your meals again.' There was not much that they could do about it though, they were just servants.

Miss Lewis and Miss Daisy absolutely denied that any of these things had happened, they even denied knowing the next two witnesses to appear. Amy Brittain and Kate Burr both testified to a life of misery, beatings and starvation under the harsh Miss Lewis. Amy had managed to escape with a small bundle of clothes after being held incommunicado for months and Kate Burr, not allowed to write or visit home, was eventually freed by her mother.

Fred appeared as a witness, as did his predecessor John Goodman, and they both said that the house was a wonderful place to live. Fred denied that he had ever been locked in the cellar and that they could always eat what ever they liked. Their evidence seemed so starkly at odds with the other testimony that the Coroner questioned them closely but to no avail. Miss Lewis, questioned as to her motives for hiring the children, simply said it was 'her hobby'. The coroner had to return an open verdict. He was very unhappy about the evidence of the two boys, Miss Lewis and Miss Daisy, but had no indication of any crime as yet. The police, watched by all of Birmingham's newspapers, needed more to go on.

It soon transpired that the police had already been called to the house to investigate allegations that both Fred and John had been mistreated. The National Society for the Prevention of Cruelty to Children took up the case on behalf of Emma Freeman and a new inquest was set for April.

Miss Lewis failed to attend. Her solicitor blithely informed the coroner that he did not think she would attend as the summons was not in order. A warrant for the arrest of Miss Lewis was issued and the meeting was adjourned for a week. Detectives were instructed to find the woman. The following week they still had not found her, but Miss Daisy had put up the contents of the house for sale.

The final inquest opened and was adjourned. Miss Florence Louise Lewis was not present. Rumour had it that she boarded a ship bound for America the previous Friday. The detectives never managed to find her; she may have got away with murder.

CHAPTER 16

The Birmingham Canal Mystery
1901
*He stood on what he thought was a dead
dog in a sack ...*

Saturday 10 August 1901 was the day on which railway Detective Thomas Hibbs died. Hibbs was employed as the night watchman at the London & North Western Railway Yard at Curzon Street. It was not the easiest of jobs as the yard was beside a very run down part of the city and pilfering of coal and other goods was a constant problem. Almost every night, gangs would sneak in and try to make off with anything not secured and they were not above threatening the railway staff with violence if they intervened. Despite this the railway company would not pay for their watchmen to go about in pairs.

Indeed, the night before, Thomas had been chasing a gang about the sidings after they had tried to break into the coal merchant's office. He very nearly caught them too, but they rounded on him, threatened to kill him and made off into the night. This happened at the end of the yard known as Paddy's Bank, right beside the canal. Once off duty Thomas returned home to get some rest.

Thomas Hibbs and his wife lived with his brother William at Nineveh, Handsworth. Both brothers

Another fight on the railway sidings.
The Strand Magazine

worked for the railway company. Thomas was a fit, strong twenty-three-year-old man and an excellent swimmer. The two of them caught the six-thirty-seven train into New Street on the Saturday evening to report for duty at Inspector Neale's office. William went off to his duties at Monument Station. At seven-twenty Thomas left the New Street Office and walked down to Curzon Street. There he met George Pratt, the gate keeper about seven-forty and went to his office to sign in and start his patrol. Shortly afterwards he met John Woodward, a loading inspector and they exchanged a few pleasantries. Thomas Hibbs then set off across Siding Number 22 towards Paddy's Bank. John Woodward was the last known person to see him alive.

At about eight Ada Grayley was standing on Fazeley Street Bridge when a drunken man bumped into her, apologised and lurched off down the towpath. It was James Lea. James was a rag and bone man and he had spent the day gathering old bits

Fellows Morton & Clayton Wharf, where David Roper alighted from the steamer Earl *just as the fight was taking place.* The Author

of rubbish around the city on his handcart. As it was Saturday his round included quite a few pubs. Not surprisingly for a warm August day, he had had the odd half pint in most of them. His favourite tipple was 'Four Penny Ale', notorious for its strength. He was pretty much leathered, as the phrase has it. His face was as black as the soot he had on his cart and he decided he needed to freshen up so he wandered down the towpath, stripped off his clothes and dived off a footbridge into the cut. He had done this before, and been sentenced to a month in prison for indecent exposure. This time such niceties went out of the window. He stood on what he thought must be a dead dog in a sack, but on diving down again, dragged up the still warm body of Thomas Hibbs. He started yelling for help, the body was too heavy for him to lift out and he was stuck there trying to hold Hibbs's head out of the water.

David Roper was walking along the towpath. He was a jobbing boat blacksmith who also sold windlasses and pulley blocks. He had just returned from mending a boat at Hatton by the fast steamer *Earl*. The steamer stopped at the Fellows, Morton and Clayton wharf not far away and David had to walk the rest of the route into the city. He knew the area was rather dangerous and so he was quietly terrified when he had to walk past a naked man about to dive into the canal. At some distance beyond he heard James's cry for help and turned back. By the time he got back some other people had arrived. They managed to get the body onto the towpath and attempted artificial respiration. About twenty or thirty women were converging on the scene too, so James Lea decided it would be a wise policy to clear off and get dressed.

Ada Grayley heard the shouts and turned to Fazeley Street where she met Henry Palmer and told him about the cries and how she had seen a drunk going down to the water. She was convinced it was the drunk who had fallen into the canal. Henry raced down the towpath, and returned a few minutes later. 'We've just pulled a man out of the water, go fetch the Police'. He returned to the scene and continued to try to get Hibbs breathing again.

By now quite a crowd was surrounding the two young men trying to revive Hibbs. Young Edward Gorman, a sixteen-year-

Birmingham & Fazeley Canal, the scene of Thomas Hibbs' last moments. Marks of a scuffle were found on the grass and towpath cinders. The Author

old local lad, commented on the watch and chain that was on Hibbs' waistcoat. A minute or two later one of the young men gave up attempting to revive Hibbs, took the watch and chain saying, 'That'll do for the coppers' and disappeared into the crowd. Neither watch, chain nor man were seen again.

A short while before this drama, Daniel Duffell, the toll collector at Fazeley Street lock, had noticed a young man walking along the towpath carrying a bag of what looked suspiciously like coal, although any concerns were soon forgotten by all the hullabaloo that followed. David Roper had left the scene fairly quickly and paused to tell Daniel what he had seen: 'I never seen such a thing in my life, a man jumped off the bridge and come up wi' a dead 'un'. Knowing the dark reputation of the area, David decided to get away before night fell.

David Roper had left the steamboat Earl at the Fellows Morton and Clayton canal basin. From the time he stepped off the boat it took a further 15 minutes for the crew to tow it into the basin to be re-coaled. The night watchmen there, Thomas Quiney, reported seeing a gang of four or five youths running along the towpath as the boat was being moored up.

Another night watchman, George Wallis, at the Corporation Interception Works, found two young men knocking at the gate by the canal. They asked him if he was going to go and help the man in the canal. George knew nothing about this, so simply bade them Goodnight. He bumped into the pair again when he went to get a jug of beer from the pub at the corner of Montague Street and Great Barr Street. He was deeply

Warwick & Birmingham Canal: James Lea dived off this bridge to freshen up, only to discover the lifeless corpse of Thomas Hibbs. The Author

suspicious of them because unless they had scaled one of the yard fences, there was no way that they could have got there in the time available. The whole area was so anarchic at the time that few of the youths there paid any attention to fences or private property. This pair looked very much like a couple of the Montague Street Peakies, one of the local street gangs.

PC Whitty arrived and arranged for Thomas Hibbs to be taken to Duke Street. The neighbourhood settled down for its usual Saturday night, with an extra item for the gossips. PC Street actually dived into the canal to search and found Hibbs handcuffs close by. They should have been attached to his belt. His truncheon was missing too.

Detective Inspector Davis of the Birmingham Police searched the area and found a bag of coal leaning against the towpath wall, as well as lumps of coal scattered around. There were quite a few scuffmarks in the towpath cinders and on the grassy verge. It looked as though Hibbs had disturbed some one, or possibly a gang, stealing coal from the goods yard. With the light failing he returned to Duke Street to try and find out why Thomas Hibbs was dead.

Dr Kennedy was acting Police Surgeon for this shift. He examined the body and discovered that Hibbs had not simply drowned; there was a large round wound to the back of his head. This had caused a slight fracture and would have undoubtedly knocked him unconscious. There was a ragged edge to the cut which had pieces of coal dust stuck to it. Hibbs had a bruise over his eye and had bitten into his tongue. There was another bruise in the small of his back. The evidence pointed to a fight in which Hibbs had been punched a few times and had then been hit hard on the head with a lump of coal. The blow knocked him out and he either fell, or was pushed into the canal. This blow had not killed him outright, and could possibly have been treated if he had been taken to hospital quickly enough. It was the water that finished him off. The coroner decided that foul play was involved, and the police start their hunt for the murderers.

At first light on the Sunday the search of the towpath began in detail. Some way from the point where Hibbs's body was found, his truncheon was spotted floating in the water. Apart

Warwick Bar: the junction of the Warwick & Birmingham Canal and the Birmingham Canals, this whole area was prey to gangs of young men known as 'Peakies'. The Author

from another bag, the same type as was found containing coal the previous day, there seemed to be no other clues. Interviews with other people at the coal yard revealed that the worst of the gangs engaged in pilfering the coal was one known as The Montague Street Peakies. They were a bunch of unruly youths sporting the 'Peaky' style haircut and renowned in the district for their violent attitude.

By Tuesday some leads started to appear after the press coverage. A letter arrived at Duke Street Station:

Private further information later, Watch G. Preston height about 7 foot and a half. Brown eyes and hair, concerned in the detective murder, by one who knows. You will see him at the Stork Hotel Corporation Street.

The next day a further letter arrived:

Dear Sir, you have as yet thrown no light on the detective murder. From information I have received I have every reason to believe George Preston of the Stork Hotel, Corporation Street, has helped in the foul crime. I am watching him all the time and this is his description, about seven feet and a half-inch, brown hair and eyes, scar on the left eye and slim. Was in Paddy's Bank at the time the crime was committed. Do not miss this chance. Signed by one who can get him hung. P. M.
P.S. He is employed as Boots.

Inspector Davis wasted no time in getting to the *Stork Hotel*. George Preston was duly interviewed and it transpired that he was not the murderer at all, but the author of the letters, accusing himself of the murder. He could not even give a reason for why he had done such a stupid thing. He was told not to do such a silly thing again and dismissed.

With the investigation back to square one, Inspector Davis had no leads at all and waited to see what would appear on the grapevine. It was not long before the city gossip started to throw up some tentative lines of enquiry. He received at tip from Harry Russell, the manager of the Great Western Hall Club at Small Heath. He said that William Billingsley had come into the club at half six in the morning a couple of days after the murder and when Harry asked him what all the police were doing down his way he said,

It served the bleeder right, he should not have gone interfering. I was not gambling, I was standing looking on, somebody said 'eh up – here comes a copper. Somebody else said, let him come, we'll do him in, we'll cut him. Then there was a scuffle of copper and candles and men.
Billingsley said he edged away.

Later on Billingsley had a similar conversation with Frank Spiers. Word got back to Inspector Davis and Detective Inspector Moron went to interview Billingsley. He admitted that he had spoken to someone who claimed to have struck

Hibbs and thrown him in the canal. The result was that Billingsley was arrested and taken into custody. Billingsley was admitting nothing but from his careless gossip it seemed that Thomas Hibbs had interrupted a gang playing cards in the dark corners under Fazeley Street Bridge. This could tally with the comments from the signalman on the railway who said that he often saw candles burning there at night. It bore little relevance to the apparent coal thefts however.

The next day Inspector Davis received more information that led to two more arrests. Frank Parslow and Charlie Webb were hauled in on the evidence of Frank's half sister's husband, Albert McCulloch. He stated that Frank had admitted to him that he had killed the detective and that his friend Charlie Webb assisted him. It all sounded very convincing; Frankie had told Albert how they were stealing coal when Hibbs caught them and that as he tried to handcuff them, a fight broke out resulting in the fatal blow with a lump of coal and Hibbs drowning. Frank Parslow was arrested at his house, and completely denied any involvement in the business.

Charlie Webb was also arrested at home. He too denied any involvement and insisted that he had been in Broad Street all day and evening, selling collar studs.

With no other leads to go on Billingsley, Parslow and Webb were brought to trial for the murder of Thomas Hibbs. The evidence was sketchy and the stories of the three accused were mutually inconsistent. The evidence of Albert McCulloch was not corroborated by any other members of the family and was thrown out. Even his wife denied hearing the conversation when she was supposed to be in the same room at the time. Billingsley may indeed have known what had happened, possibly even been involved but there was no substantive evidence against him except hearsay. The charges against all three were dropped.

Inspector Davis never did find out who killed Thomas Hibbs. The violent gangs that terrorised the neighbourhood ensured no one came forward with any more evidence.

CHAPTER 17

The Price Street Killing
1901
... Joyce pulled out the knife and plunged it into the old man's chest, straight into his heart.

Price Street, to the north-east of the city centre, was one of the sprawling slums generated by the Industrial Revolution. Crowded into jerry built courtyards of flimsy buildings were a mix of decent, hard working but poorly paid families and some of the dross at the very bottom of the social scale. It was a mixture that threw up a constant catalogue of tragedy.

The Nugent family lived in a typical slum house: 9, the court, behind No 6 house, Price Street.

Elizabeth and John Nugent, were getting on in years. John was sixty-one, quite an achievement in itself considering the ghastly working conditions of the time. He was now fairly frail and earned his keep as a bamboo worker; cutting and weaving imported bamboo for furniture. Elizabeth was somewhat stronger, although we don't know whether she went out to work as well. They had several sons, the oldest of whom, Michael, aged twenty-nine, still lived at home. Michael seems to have had some mental problems, not serious enough to stop him working, but he had difficulty expressing himself clearly. He had already spent some time in Winson Green Asylum.

In 1899 Michael had met John 'Toby' Joyce in the *White Hart*, Bagot Street. Joyce had just arrived in the city after working briefly in Southampton Docks. He had recently finished nine years service in the army. There he had been posted on the North West Frontier of India, not quite as dangerous as Southern Africa, but still a hot spot at the edge of the Empire. He was a man described by the *Birmingham Daily Post* as 'particularly ill favoured, vicious looking fellow, with close set eyes, and the scars of several frays on his head.'

Heaven only knows why, but Michael invited Joyce back to his home for a meal. It may have started off as a friendly reception to life in Birmingham, but during the meal something started an argument between Michael and Joyce that ended up with furniture being broken and the start of a nasty feud between Joyce and the whole Nugent family. Joyce was later to say that both men, wielding pokers and knives, had attacked him although Joyce seemed to have a very selective and creative memory when put to the question.

Despite his handicap, Michael managed to have a steady job. It seems that he was something of a loner, with few friends outside the family, and had to walk home after being paid at work alone. This did not go un-noticed by some of the unemployed yobs that infested the slum. Joyce had slipped into this mob with little difficulty and seems to have been involved in several incidents where Michael was robbed of his wages. Michael started taking a poker with him on his journey to and from work. The muggings stopped even if the simmering feud did not.

Matters blew up on 28 May 1901 when two friends of Joyce, Treeney and Kelly, attacked Michael outside the court. Joyce was on the outskirts of the scrap. Duffy, another resident of the court, waded in to help Michael. Joyce joined in and fists and knives were flying everywhere. The fracas flared up again in the evening, and this time Michael's brother, Thomas, became involved as well. The police arrived and they were all hauled off to either the hospital or police station. The row continued in the hospital and Thomas was ordered to leave. The following day Joyce, Kelly and Treeney were charged with assault and brought before the magistrate. The evidence required to convict them had to be presented by Michael. Michael was unable to present a coherent account of the events and consequently the charges were dropped.

The feud between Joyce and the Nugent's stepped up a notch. Joyce started hanging around the court at the back of No 6. On 8 June he told Thomas Nugent he would do him in.

The next day he told Emma Moore, who also lived there, 'I shall get my own back with them. I'll get five years, but I'll get my own back.'

In the cramped confines of the squalid court things came to a head a day later. Joyce had been drinking for most of 10 June. Bitter and, vengeful, he turned up at the court at about six in the evening. Emma Moore asked him what he was doing and he mumbled some excuse and hung about on the street, occasionally wandering into the court until around ten. He barged into the Nugent's apartment and Emma, fearing some trouble, went in after him. Michael was not there so Joyce rounded on his father and started abusing him. After a few minutes of this he picked up a paraffin lamp and smashed it at John's feet. Luckily the whole house did not go up in flames but Elizabeth grabbed Joyce and pinned his arms to the wall, shouting for her husband to get out and call the police. John left as fast as his old legs could carry him. Struggling with Emma and Elizabeth, Joyce managed to rip himself free by threatening to bite off Elizabeth's nose. She had noticed a knife concealed up his sleeve.

Outside, John Nugent had barely managed to reach the street when Joyce caught up with him. In a fierce but brief struggle Joyce pulled out the knife and plunged it into the old man's chest, straight into his heart. A bunch of Joyce's friends were hanging around outside the yard. Elizabeth ran after Joyce but two girls in the group shoved her to the ground. Joyce sneered at her, saying 'If you were not an old lady I'd serve you the same.' He ran off down Price Street and passed the knife to one of his cronies, James Clifford.

His reputation as a vicious thug and the dozens of witnesses to the stabbing ensured that Joyce was rapidly tracked down and arrested. In court he wheedled and distorted the entire story, but even with a very good defence lawyer, the jury took just over an hour to find him guilty. The Judge donned his black cap and passed the death sentence on him. During the trial he had claimed that his service in India had caused him to suffer sunstroke and that meant that he suffered temporary lapses of consciousness. It was a pretty flimsy excuse, but the defence lawyer made the most of it and the jury's verdict was returned with a plea for mercy if it was proved that he had suffered brain damage from the sunstroke. The judge seemed rather sceptical that it would turn out that way. He was right to be dubious. None of the doctors that attended Joyce reported any such mental impairment. It meant not five years for some vicious attack, but the gallows for the wilful murder of a frail old man.

On 20 August, Mr Billington, the state executioner, arrived, this time with his son. It was a family business after all. The gallows at Warwick Prison had not been used for five years, so he tested it with a sand bag that evening. Satisfied that it was in full working order, the Billingtons slept peacefully through the night. Joyce probably did not, since the sound of them testing the trap door and gibbet with a bag the same weight as him was taking place only yards from his cell. At ten to eight the next day Joyce was dressed and escorted the short walk to the gallows. In a few moments he was dead. Outside a crowd of well over 3,000 watched the black flag raised on a clear warm August morning.

CHAPTER 18

The Smethick Mystery
1902
... he was buried with due respect and with a properly-named headstone.

On 20 September 1902 a body was pulled out of the canal at Galton Bridge. It was that of an old man, roughly 70 years old. The man had a prominent nose and high forehead, balding but with whiskers, but with nothing to identify him, his demise only attracted a small note in the papers. He had not drowned, but seems to have had a heart attack and fallen in. There were no suspicious circumstances and the case raised little comment; just another unfortunate man.

There was just one unusual feature mentioned; in his jacket was a specially sewn pocket that contained a spoon. At first no one came forward to identify the body and, with no clue as to

The complex of canals near Galton Bridge saw mixture of tragedy and farce when the body of an old man was found in the water here. The Author

its identity, the coroner arranged for the nameless man to be given a paupers funeral at the Uplands Cemetery, all at the expense of the city.

After the inquest, and just before the funeral, a family appeared and thought that the man might possibly be their father who had gone away some twelve months previously. Indeed, six of them turned up to view the body, including the man's daughter and son-in-law. They all agreed that it was indeed Francis Poultney of Ladywood Road, Birmingham. Mr Poultney had always earned his living as a stone-cutter and frequently travelled away from home for long periods in search of work. It was this itinerant life style that had made his daughter sow an extra pocket into his jacket so that he could easily keep his own spoon for eating from communal pots of stew or at soup kitchens. All six relatives swore an affidavit that the corpse was Mr Francis Poultney. It was a bit late to change the funeral arrangements, so he was buried with due respect and with a properly-named headstone. The death certificate was amended to give the correct name and that seemed to be that. An insurance policy on the man paid out £50 pounds and the dust settled on the affair.

On Saturday 1 November there was a knock on the daughter's front door, not long before midnight. The mourning family's daughter opened the door and promptly had a fit of hysterics; there stood Mr Francis Poultney. The daughter and son-in-law came down stairs and the son said, 'We buried you a month ago' to which he got the reply 'Well the lid was not strong enough,' which probably did not help the daughter recover her wits one little bit.

It seems that despite the spoon, they had identified the wrong old man; Francis Poultney was alive and well, and sprightly for a seventy-year-old. He managed to cadge the price of a train fare to Hanley from them so that he could get a job there and left after a couple of days. The insurance money had to be paid back and to this day it remains a mystery as to who was the body in the canal. Everyone seemed grateful that at least they hadn't had the time to bury the unknown man in the family tomb alongside Mrs Poultney. Apparently she would have been furious.

CHAPTER 19

The Sparkbrook Tragedy
1902
She returned upstairs and, sitting in front of the dressing table mirror, cut her own throat.

At what point does a mother finally snap? After the death one child? Or two, perhaps three? Annie Louisa Collins had lost four children by 1902. She was married to Thomas Collins, who made brass lamps for trains and ships, and they had one surviving son, William John, who was five. They lived at 44 Leamington Road, Sparkbrook.

In July 1901 Annie's grip on reality was starting to loosen. She became convinced that she had drowned a child in the brook in Stoney Lane. She had not, and her husband decided that it was time to get her to a doctor. Charles Weekes examined her and thought that it would be best if she was locked up in an asylum. Thomas at first agreed, but the next day told the doctor that it would not be a good idea and

Stoney Lane, Sparkbrook. Annie Collins hallucinated that she had drowned her child in the brook in this lane. John Marks Collection

refused to allow her to go. Although the doctor did not know at the time, Annie's brother was already in an asylum and presumably Thomas knew how bad the conditions were in such places.

In place of the asylum treatment Thomas managed to get her to go and stay with her brother out in the country at Kings Heath. She stayed there for a couple of months and made a reasonable recovery. Unfortunately only a short while after she returned to the house at Leamington Road, she heard the sad news that her brother in the asylum had died. Thomas bought some medicine from the doctor that helped, but she was very withdrawn from that day on.

Mrs Jesson, who lived next door at No 46, had heard quarrels from time to time. Indeed on Coronation Night the row had got so loud that she sent her son round to make the peace. On 19 July 1902 she was called in by Thomas to see Annie because he thought she had drunk something. She found Annie being violently sick in the kitchen. Annie had drunk a poison called Condy's Fluid. She seemed to recover and said that the worry about the doctor's bills had upset her. She hugged Thomas and said it would be all right. Mrs Jesson was worried and made Annie some warm milk to ease her stomach. She called back again at nine that night to see that everything was all right. William John was asleep in bed and Thomas and Annie seemed very happy together.

The next morning Mrs Jesson called, but the doors were locked and there was no answer. By lunchtime she was seriously worried and contacted Annie's sister. There was still no answer from the house so they called a policeman to force the door.

Downstairs everything was just as she had left it the night before. The policeman and the two women went upstairs. The front bedroom door would not open at first, but when the constable pushed hard, Annie's body fell away from it and they got in. She had cut her throat with a pocketknife. Lying on the bed was Thomas, his head battered to pieces. Sadder by far, in the back bedroom young William John lay dead, his head pushed into the pillow until he had suffocated.

The Constable searched further. In the kitchen Annie had tried to clean the meat cleaver that she had used on her

One last kiss. The Strand Magazine

husband, and got out all the life insurance policies, leaving bloody fingerprints over them. She returned upstairs and, sitting in front of the dressing table mirror, cut her own throat. Bleeding heavily, she walked around to her side of the bed but collapsed to the floor in front of the door before she could lie beside her husband for the last time.

CHAPTER 20

The Inge Street Murder of a Prostitute
1903
'Don't let me go home tonight, he will murder me.'

Edwardian society was remarkably coy about some aspects of life. A polite veil was drawn over the more unsavoury parts of Birmingham and, unless they hit the headlines, places like Inge Street were left to get on with it. Inge Street was described as the 'very darkest part of Birmingham' and words failed the genteel when it came to describing what went on around the back of such streets. The killing of prostitute, Martha Simpson, bought unwanted attention to the district.

Charles Dyer was an Irishman who had joined the Royal Artillery as a youth and served in India and Malta. He went on to join the Royal Warwickshire and finally left the army aged twenty-five just before Christmas 1903. He ended up in Birmingham, drinking himself into the grave and living off the earnings of the fiery tempered Martha Simpson. It was a world of casual sex and even more casual violence fuelled by alcohol and supported by the local pawnshops. They lived at No 2, at the back of No 21, Inge Street, a run down set of rooms barely deserving the title of home.

February 3rd was just another day. Martha rose late in the morning and went to see her best friend Margaret Moran, who lived in Birmingham Place off Bristol Street. Margaret lived with Arthur Lockley and John Moran, who was no relation despite the name. They all wandered back down to Inge Street where, at about seven o'clock Dyer asked the two girls to go out and pawn something. They returned with a shilling that Martha handed over to Dyer. Now that they had a bit of cash they all decamped to a pub in Old Meeting Street, via a few others en route. By eleven o'clock things were picking up.

A court. One of the few back-to-back courts that survive in Inge Street. It all looks far too clean now! The Author

Margaret Moran went off and Martha then took a man over to Birmingham Place to ply her trade.

Things started to turn nasty at Birmingham Place. Sometime later, John Moran and Arthur Lockley turned up, closely followed by Charles Dyer. Margaret's sister, Mary Ann and Alice Tatlow were also in the room. The man that Martha had entertained seems to have quietly left. Charles was in a dark mood, although no more than normal according to

The Inge Street District was one of the early housing developments. Although well built and used by skilled workers at first; it eventually became a notorious slum.
The Author

Moran and Lockley. Martha tried to get up from the armchair but Charles shoved her back down. She tried to get up again and Charles shoved her back again, this time pulling out a vicious razor saying, 'I will put this across you tonight.'

Mary Ann and Alice decided to get out. As they crossed the yard, Mary Ann heard Martha say to Margaret 'Maggie, don't let me go home tonight, he will murder me.'

Tempers must have cooled as the two girls left. Around midnight, Martha and Charles left the house in Birmingham Place and walked the couple of hundred yards back to Inge

The Queens Tavern *at the corner of Inge Street must have been one of Charles Dyers regular haunts.* The Author

Street. No one will ever know what they talked about, or argued over, as they got back to the dingy hovel they called home. Fifteen minutes later Charles burst into Margaret's house, his waistcoat undone, saying 'Oh Mag, go and save her, I have done it.'

'Done what?'

'Done her in.'

Martha, John and Arthur raced down to Inge Street. Martha was slumped in a chair, blood pouring down her chest. Her throat was cut from ear to ear. The blood soaked razor was lying on a table beside her. A poker with hair stuck to it was lying on the floor at her feet.

PC Parnham turned up at the scene of the murder while Inspector Hodgkins went to Birmingham Place with Margaret, John and Arthur. Here he found Charles Dyer in a dazed state:

'I've done it, I've cut her head off.'

'What do you mean?'

'My wife, I struck her on the head with the poker and then drew the razor across her throat'

Hodgkins arrested and charged him with murder straight away and Dyer simply said 'Correct, I plead guilty.'

The ensuing court case created a sensation, the gory details were not considered suitable for the delicate genteel Edwardian ladies to hear, not that the papers had any qualms about reporting the proceedings virtually verbatim. The courtroom was packed. Although Dyer pleaded not guilty, the sentence was quickly agreed: death by hanging. He was sent to Warwick Gaol on 17 March.

April the 5th was set for the execution. Huge crowds gathered outside the prison, but there was little to see. Public executions had been banned back in 1868, but most prisons raised a black flag when the deed was done. Now not even this symbol of justice being done was allowed. The crowds milled about until an hour after Dyer had been executed, a few warders emerged from the prison doors and stuck up a small poster stating simply that Charles Dyer had been hanged. The coroner confirmed an instantaneous death by a dislocated neck. The squalid warren around Inge Street settled back into welcome obscurity.

It was not many months before the spectre of the Inge Street killing surfaced again. If genteel society attempted to ignore the problems of poverty and prostitution; the people condemned to live in these conditions had no choice but put up with them. Their living conditions were so terrible that tempers flared with monotonous regularity. Parts of the city had to live with a constant undercurrent of violence and misery. Barely 500 yards from Inge Street lay Coventry Street. Each house had its own

Lives of poverty. Strand Magazine

yard, and each yard a warren of tiny ramshackle rooms, badly built and with little or no sanitation or services. Whole families were raised in accommodation that we would now classify as a coal shed. Children died by the score, from disease, from accidents and simply from being squashed whilst sharing a bed with the whole family.

Samuel Holden and Susan Humphries lived in one of these ghastly rooms at the back of 109 Coventry Street. Samuel, who was thirty-two had been in the army since 1890, serving both in India and South Africa. It was in South Africa that he had been wounded in the Battle of Belfontaine and was no longer fit for active duty. He left the service and settled in Birmingham at the beginning of 1904 where he managed to get a job as a market porter. People who knew him said that he was a peaceful man when sober, but short tempered after a few drinks. They said that he would do almost anything for Susan.

Susan Humphries had left her husband some time prior to this, changed her name from Annie, and made her way in the city as best she could. When she met Samuel they settled down together in a small house further along Coventry Street, living together as man and wife. Despite this, she continued to earn money by going out on the streets. Their neighbours often heard ferocious arguments and at the time of the Inge Street murder Samuel was heard to shout at her 'I'll do a Dyer on you!' Their landlady, Mrs Mary Oliver had known Susan for nearly five years and felt that Susan had just as bad a temper as Samuel. Although there were frequent quarrels Mary did not think that any harm would ever come of them.

Coventry Street. Once again the only original buildings are the pubs. The old back-to-backs have all been demolished. The Author

On 30 June the couple moved house, into a single room, in No 2, at the back of 109 Coventry Street. It was anything but a step up in the world. The house was in a courtyard of eight houses, each consisting of three rooms, one above the other, with a single door in the ground-floor kitchen. They were tiny, and each house was further subdivided into individually furnished rooms let out as bed-sits. Washing facilities were effectively non-existent and the houses shared a communal toilet in the yard.

Heaven knows what Mr & Mrs Davis thought of their new housemates; they rented the top bedroom and had to share the kitchen. Mr Davis was a labourer and so out at work most days, Martha stayed at home. On 2 July Martha was in the kitchen chatting with Sarah Taylor at teatime when Samuel came home. Not long after he went upstairs they heard a quarrel and Susan came down. She had a cut chin and complained that Samuel had hit her, and she was frightened he would kill her. Both Martha and Sarah told her to say out of his way until he had sobered up and cooled down, but it seems Susan's blood was up and she stormed back up stairs.

The row seems to have started when Samuel got back to their new flat and found that Susan had only got a plate of eggs for his meal: 'What no meat for a Saturday,' he demanded. He had given her some money to get food, and she had spent it on booze; not that he was entirely sober himself. Susan just said no, and Samuel went to hit her. He missed and she retaliated with a chair, cracking him on the head. Samuel managed to thump her on the chin before she ran off downstairs to Martha and Sarah.

It really would have been better if she had stayed in the kitchen. Upstairs Samuel managed to find a tin of sardines and was using a knife to prise it open. Across the yard at No 7 Eliza Walton was sitting in her kitchen window, and at No 8 Alice Rowen was sitting on her doorstep. Alice's husband worked with Samuel in the market. Susan had gone back upstairs and apparently had another go at Samuel with the chair. Eliza and Alice both looked up when they heard a scream. Eliza was sure that she saw Samuel strike at Susan's shoulder with a knife several times, Alice thought it was a sauce bottle, but later decided it must have been a knife. They both agreed that Susan fell forwards.

In the kitchen Sarah Taylor had left Martha alone. Samuel came down stairs.

'Fetch a doctor, I've done her in,' and he calmly walked out of the door.

Martha rushed upstairs to find Susan lying on the floor, bleeding heavily. The alarm was soon raised and a doctor, police and horse drawn ambulance arrived. They carried the bleeding and unconscious Susan to the ambulance, but she died just as they set off to the hospital.

Samuel wandered off into the city. Dazed and confused, with bloodstained hands, he trailed from one pub to another until at about seven, somewhere in Digbeth, he felt someone catch hold of his arm. It was Detective Sergeant Whitehouse.

'How is she?' She was dead, and he was arrested.

Samuel seems to have been popular with his workmates at the market. Thomas Rowen even tried to get his wife and the other witnesses to change their story, and he was severely reprimanded by the court for it. By 14 July, Samuel Holden was on trial for the murder of Susan Humphries. On 28 July he was found guilty and sentenced to death. On 16 August a familiar crowd assembled outside Warwick Prison waiting for the news of the execution. Inside, Samuel Holden asked for beer and sardines for breakfast and walked the short distance to the scaffold with a Catholic Chaplain. A few seconds later he was dead. Outside a bell tolled and a little girl was nearly crushed in the crowd.

The murder of Susan Humphries heralded a new development for the coroner. It was the first case where the growing technology of photography was used to provide incontrovertible evidence to back up witness statements. Both Eliza Walton and Alice Rowen had stated that they had seen the attack on Susan. However Alice had changed her statement from initially seeing Susan struck with a sauce bottle, to that of a knife. A question was raised as to the veracity of both statements. Detective Parrot took his camera into Mrs Walton's kitchen and got Detective Inspector Goldrick to stand in the position where Susan had been before she fell. The photograph showed that Eliza Walton could see everything that had happened. None of the rooms was fitted with the luxury of curtains.

CHAPTER 21

The Sudden and Inevitable End of Duncan Jones
1903
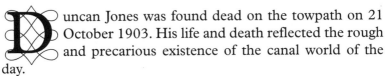
There was a pool of blood around his head and he was stone-dead.

Duncan Jones was found dead on the towpath on 21 October 1903. His life and death reflected the rough and precarious existence of the canal world of the day.

Duncan had a fearsome reputation. He was a big man, working as a coal-heaver required strength and stamina since the boats carried twenty-five tons of coal and it had to be manhandled out of the hold. It was filthy and gruelling work, hundredweight blocks of lump coal or huge shovels of slack had to be lifted five or six feet until all twenty-five tons was unloaded. It did not even pay very well and Duncan was technically of no fixed abode, although he often spent time with his girlfriend Rose Burgess of Pope Street. At thirty-one years old he had never gained enough savings to contemplate marriage. In fact most of his wages seemed to have gone on beer; and he tended to be very quarrelsome after a few pints. By the start of October 1903 he had been in custody thirty-six times, mostly for assault, and this did not stop him smashing a quart jug over another labourer's head. The man, Ixon by name, had to be dragged semi-conscious to hospital. A few days later Duncan Jones threw another man in the canal and pelted him with stones as he struggled to save himself.

Shortly after midnight, on 21 October Harry Rabone, the night watchman at Knyoch's in Lodge Road heard a scream, and then some called 'Murder!' at least four times. He ran up the embankment to the canal wall, but could see nothing in the dark. He then heard a chilling sound, 'like the kicking of a horse'. George Crimshaw, a metal annealer who also worked at Kynoch's and had come with Rabone, thought it was more like a thumping sound. George ran to get the police and in the ensuing silence Harry heard the footsteps of someone running away. PC Raven arrived with George and they found the battered body of Duncan Jones lying on his back on the towpath near Lodge Bridge. There was a pool of blood around his head and he was stone-dead. PC Raven had little trouble identifying Jones; with his record all the local police knew exactly who he was.

A few days after throwing the man in the canal, Duncan Jones had first demanded and then taken food from the tommy bucket on the boat run by William Coggins and George Plant. George was just getting a couple of bags of fodder from the stable when Jones grabbed the food. William said

'Wait till my mate gets back and see what he will give you.'

'**** your mate, and if you say two words about this you'll go in the cut,' Jones replied.

Hockley Port. As the fight between the boatmen happened, the boat was blown across the canal into this basin, nearly pulling the boat horse into the water. The Author

George returned and berated William for letting Jones take the food but Tommy Phillips who was helping them that night said 'I know what he is, he would kill a man as soon as look at him.' Tommy would not even have the food that had been near Jones's hand in the bucket. Tommy should know; he was at the *Shakespeare* pub when Jones split open Ixon's head. For the next fortnight Jones went round saying he would 'do for' George Plant and William Coggins. An air of simmering feud surrounded the wharves of Soho Loop and Hockley Port .

On Tuesday the 20th various boats were getting ready for the coal run the following morning. Hockley Port was one of the main ports for coal and always busy with boats, day and night. The wharves extended beneath Lodge Road towards Park Road, surrounded by stables and canal workers houses. Thomas Phillips and Duncan Jones were to crew one boat whilst George Plant and William Coggins were on another. Phillips and Jones worked on their boat until seven-thirty pm and then for another hour in Mr Bowater's stables. Once all was ready they walked up the towpath and Jones left Phillips at the corner of Roseberry Street to go and see his girlfriend Rose. Thomas walked to the *Canal Tavern*. They were going to met up again at eleven, sleep on the boat and get off to an early start about half four the next morning. In the *Canal Tavern* Thomas met William and George who had similar plans. An hour later all three of them walked back down to the boats to get some rest.

Duncan had gone to see Rose. It was her birthday, and they went to the *Mint* pub to celebrate. They chatted away. Duncan was worried that Ixon planned to get revenge on him, apparently he had threatened him and was 'carrying a piece of cold steel for him.' It was going to be an early start the next day, so Rose gave Duncan a piece of ham for his lunch and watched him walk down Pope Street towards the canal just after eleven o'clock. Thomas Phillips was now asleep in his boat, but at half-eleven he was roused by the sound of another boat slipping quietly past his. It was William and George, casting off early to get ahead of the morning rush, quite possibly to get some distance between them and the notorious Duncan Jones as well. Thomas nodded off again only to woken fifteen minutes later by a piercing scream, as if by a woman. He looked out of the cabin but saw nothing, and returned to his slumbers.

The only witnesses to the following events were George and William. William led the boat horse as George poled the boat into the channel away from Wharf Street and towards Lodge Road Bridge, heading down the Soho Loop towards the Birmingham Canal Main Line. William recalled the scene; as the horse, some twenty yards ahead of the boat, passed beneath the bridge, who should appear on the path but Duncan Jones.

'Hello you ****, I have catched you, and there is going to be a **** row if you don't give me something to eat.'

William said he could not spare anything; they only had one tommy bucket and would have to wait for the loading. Duncan said he was going to have some anyway and then punched William on the nose. William punched him right back. Duncan went to the boat and said to George,

'Hallo you **** big ****, I'm going to do you in.' He jumped onto the boat and wrenched the tiller out of the helm, swinging it across George's back, knocking him to the deck.

Lodge Road Branch. The body of Duncan Jones was found on the canal towpath to the left of the picture. Kynoch's factory was just behind the wall. The Author

George hit him back hard and Duncan jumped back off the boat with the tiller, but George followed him and they wrestled for the tiller. The wind had now caught the boat, blowing it towards the railway basins and threatening to drag the horse into the canal. William managed to catch the horse and regain control of the boat. George grabbed the tiller and leapt back. They got away from the scene as fast as the boat could go.

As daylight showed the extent of Duncan's injuries it was clear that he had died from a single massive blow to the head and arm, inflicted with something not dissimilar to a boat tiller. 'Extraordinary violence' was the doctor's comment. Thomas Phillips was roused from his boat at four and the word quickly went out for the arrest of William and George. Inspector Marshall received a telephone message, and went to Holly Bank Colliery in Short Heath. There he found the two men waiting for their boat to be loaded. They were arrested, examined and interviewed. Neither of them showed any sign of bruising, despite their accounts of the previous night. George said that it was he that had cried murder and if someone had come to help, none of this would have happened. George went on, 'We killed him, if we hadn't, he would have killed us. If I get the rope, I can't help it.'

They were charged with manslaughter since there did not seem to be evidence for a murder charge. By now the bruises from the fight started to show on George, across his hips and shoulders, giving credence to his account. The case came to court a month later, and the jury determined that William and George had acted to save their own lives. They walked free from the court, the nightmare of bully Duncan Jones finally over.

CHAPTER 22

The Perils of Childhood

... Inspector Gosling burst in on the funeral party and stopped it just as they were nailing the lid on the coffin.

Growing up in turn of the century Birmingham was a pretty perilous business. Simply avoiding the many childhood diseases was a matter of luck, even though the city had invested heavily in clean water and proper sewage disposal. The perils started even before birth.

The Victorians believed that abortion was wrong. Although not quite murder, it was still a crime and distinctly frowned upon. The result was that there was a trade in back street abortion that killed thousands of unborn infants, and quite a few of their mothers too.

Rumours reached the City Coroner that something was not quite right about the death of Mrs Jeannie Siviter. It took them several days to find out just who she was and where her body lay. It created a huge scandal when Inspector Gosling burst in on the funeral party and stopped it just as they were nailing the lid on the coffin. Another couple of hours and he would have been too late. The body was removed to the mortuary. The investigation was to open up the world of back street abortions, and have a peculiar twist in it as well.

Mrs Siviter used to be Mrs Cook. She had eight children when Mr Cook died, which was quite enough of a handful before having another child by her new husband, Mr Siviter in 1897. They had not been married long before they decided to live apart, with Mr Thomas Henry Siviter paying her maintenance and providing extra milk for the child from his dairy business. She moved to 72, Vincent Parade, Balsall Heath. Never in the best of health, she was horrified to discover that she was pregnant in December 1898.

Men of Birmingham.

INSPECTOR GOSLING.

From a Photo by Draycott, New Street.

The Coroner's right hand man, Inspector Gosling, had to stop the funeral of Mrs Siviter because of information he had received. Birmingham Gazette

At first Jeanie seems to have tried some special potions provided by a 'doctor' in Alcester Road. These had no effect other than to make her violently sick. This was about the worst thing that could happen as she was suffering from consumption and bronchitis as well. Jeanie decided she needed an abortion. She discussed this with some of her friends, all girls naturally, and sent for the one person she thought could help ... Mrs Craven, the local midwife.

'She wants 5 shillings off me,' She complained to her friend and lodger, Mary Jane Baum, 'but unless she brings it on I shan't pay her.'

Apparently Mrs Craven had not done a thing, for a fortnight later Jeanie sent out for a boot hook, swearing she would do it herself. This idea lost its appeal, no doubt at the sight of the boot hook and Mrs Craven was called back several times. The midwife was wise enough to realise that Jeanie was now seriously ill from consumption and the stress of an abortion would probably kill her. She refused to perform the operation. Christmas passed with an increasingly sick and worried Jeanie looking for any method to terminate her pregnancy. The consumption was infecting her liver by now and the doctor became a regular visitor.

Most of Jeanie's friends thought that Mrs Craven had actually performed the operation. Jeanie died on 7 April, Dr Hickie arrived for his weekly visit just after she took her last breath and he certified that she had died of phthisis. Her lungs were destroyed by the consumption and the arrangements were begun for her funeral. The gossip about Mrs Craven's treatment was intense, when her close friends were laying her out they noticed a hard lump in her abdomen, was this the result of a botched abortion? Rumours reached the Coroner's Office.

Inspector Gosling and Detective Inspector Daniels went to stop the funeral whilst Detective Sergeant Moxon raced around to 45 Jakeman Street and arrested Rebecca Craven on suspicion of performing an illegal operation.

Mrs Craven's future depended on the result of the autopsy. She swore she had done nothing to Jeanie. The result surprised everyone. Not only was there no trace of an abortion or miscarriage, Jeanie was not even pregnant. The disease had probably stopped her normal cycle, and that had been enough to convince her she was pregnant. She need never have worried. The hard lump that worried her friends was an inflamed liver.

St Lukes Road. Mrs Louisa Hillier lived in this street, practising illegal abortions for 5 shillings each. John Marks Collection

A decade later Mrs Zambra certainly was pregnant. She already had five children and on her husband's slim wages working as a waiter, she really did not need another one. On 11 May 1910 Mary Zambra went with her sister in law, Jane, to see Mrs Louisa Hillier at her home in St Lukes Road. It was the third time Mary had been to see her. On the first two occasions Mrs Hillier had talked her out of the idea of terminating the pregnancy, but this time Jane had to wait whilst Mrs Hillier took Mary into another room to do the operation. She asked Mary if her husband knew about it and she said 'Yes, he has given me five shillings to come with.'

A week later Charles Zambra got home at eleven-thirty. The lights were on and there were two women in the house, Mrs Hillier and Mrs Lander. Mrs Lander he knew was his wife's close friend but he had never met Mrs Hillier. His wife was dreadfully ill, she had just had a miscarriage. After a short while Charles insisted on calling for Dr Sims. Mrs Hillier was not impressed, 'If Dr Sims sees me it will be all up with me. He knows me.' And with that she left the house hurriedly.

Dr Sims arrived at one-thirty the next morning. He did not find anything to unduly worry him, but over the next week Mary became steadily more ill with septic pneumonia. On the Monday a feverish Mary held tightly onto her husband, 'Charles, I have done you wrong. I was mad. I have gambled with my life and I have got to pay the penalty.'

She died at six-forty on 23 April.

A warrant was issued for the arrest of Mrs Hillier. Detective Inspector Goldrick managed to track her down to Blackfriars in London. He brought her back by train to face the inquest.

The problem for the doctors was that there was little that they could prove apart from the fact that there had been a miscarriage and subsequent infection. Whether the miscarriage was artificially induced was impossible to prove with the technology of the day. Mrs Hillier walked free from the court, although her reputation was in tatters.

Getting born was certainly not the end to the dangers that faced children. Most deliveries were at home, without even the assistance of a midwife. Consequently there was a large number of still births and deaths among the newly born. The coroner must have sometimes become sad at the inquest of yet another unknown infant found wrapped in an old cloth and dumped in the canal. The cost of a funeral was well beyond the means of its family.

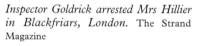
Inspector Goldrick arrested Mrs Hillier in Blackfriars, London. The Strand Magazine

Child neglect had to be pretty dire before it attracted any real attention. The moral code of the time really did expect children to be seen and not heard, work hard and be respectful of their elders who would look after them. The children did not always live up to this high standard … what a surprise! The adults were not always as diligent parents as they should be either. Mary Jane Onslow was really not the sort of person you would want as your parent.

Harry Onslow failed to spot just how hopeless his wife was at raising their three children. He worked as a warehouseman at the Battery Company Works in Selly Oak, leaving home at four in the morning and not usually returning until after nine at night, six days a week. His usual wages amounted to around 21 shillings and with this he bought the groceries, paid the rent and such like. He had learned that it was not a good idea to give it to Mary. She had a tendency to drink, 'breaking out' was the way Harry described it.

They lived in one furnished room in one of the myriad courts at the back of Allison Street. These miserable houses had been jerry built through the mid nineteenth century and offered cheap but awful accommodation for the vast mass of workers in the new industries. The city corporation was trying to buy them up and demolish them to make way for cleaner, more substantial housing. One aspect of these courts was that the close proximity of all the neighbours helped create a small community that could, to a limited degree, look after its weaker members. This was all long before social services and the modern array of welfare services. There was a Society for the Prevention of Cruelty to Children and their inspectors managed to catch some of the worst abuses but they had fairly restricted powers.

Mary Jane Onlsow was well-known to the local Inspector. He had called round frequently in 1899 trying to persuade Mary to take better care of her children. The youngest daughter, Agnes May, was clearly failing to thrive, at twenty months old she was barely half her normal weight and emaciated. Priscilla Kay, one of their neighbours, had seen Agnes left alone in the yard all day, dressed in one tatty garment and looking very poorly. The child was dumped in

Daily Argus.

MONDAY, OCTOBER 9, 1899.

CHARGE AGAINST A BIRMINGHAM
MOTHER.

THE INQUEST.

MARY ANN ONSLOW.

Mary Ann Onslow was pilloried in the press as a wicked mother and a drunkard. Today we may have replaced one type of drug for another, but the problems remain the same. Daily Argus

the yard again the next day and Priscilla called in the Inspector.

Mary regularly went on drinking binges. The Inspector called around in August and found the children alone in the room. When he asked where their mother was, the two oldest boys took him round to the *British Lion Inn* in Digbeth. She was thoroughly drunk and gave him a torrent of abuse. He was not impressed. All the children were dirty and half starved and the room was absolutely filthy. The August Bank Holiday saw Mary going on another bender. She became so drunk that she fell over in the street and knocked herself out on the pavement. The children were placed in the workhouse while she recovered in the infirmary.

Inspector Holmes called round on 7 September to find the room a shambles, the children still no better treated and Mary slumped in a chair, half dressed and sporting a black eye. He found that Agnes was dressed in only a couple of garments and was terribly thin. He asked Mary how this state of affairs came about but she shrugged and said they were perfectly all right. Mrs Cave, the landlady, was in the room at the time and snorted with derision, 'The reason why they are so neglected is that you are always drinking.' Mary denied this and said her neighbours were ill-treating her to get her into trouble.

This was hardly true. Kate Clark had taken Agnes into her home and cared for her when Mary went out on a two-day bender. Leah Terry, another neighbour, had done much the same. The day before the inspector's visit, their patience finally ran out and all the women of the court grabbed Mary and gave her a traditional ducking in the horse trough to buck her ideas up.

The ducking brought about some improvement. For a couple of weeks Mary looked after the children reasonably well, but for little Agnes it was not enough to remedy the long term starvation. On 1 October Mary took Agnes to Dr Murphy, who prescribed some medicine to be taken with milk and port wine. It was too good to last though and Mary went off on another drinking binge for three days, leaving the children with no food or fire. Kate Clark, Rose Lee and the others did what they could for the children out of pity, but they had little enough to be able to share. It was now 5 October and the children needed warmth as well as sustenance. Mary was out on yet another session.

Rose sent her daughter, Agnes, up to the Onslow's room at lunchtime with some food and drink. Agnes found the little mite moaning in pain and called her mother for help. They tried to settle her and hoped that Harry would come home from work soon.

Harry got back from work at nine-thirty. He found Agnes May dead on the bed. She was just twenty-two months old and had starved to death because of the neglect of her mother.

The dark bridges of the Birmingham and Fazeley Canal saw the disposal of many dead infants whose parents were too poor to afford a funeral. The Author

CHAPTER 23

A Gangland Shooting
1905

*Standing at the top of the steps, she faced a
milling mob of young men armed with knives,
broken bottles and swinging belts.*

O ne aspect of city life seems to have changed very
little over a century. Gangs of young men sorting
out their differences with guns, knives, bottles and
such like were just as common a hundred years ago as they are
today. They might not have had automatic sub-machine guns
and an expensive drug habit, but the results were pretty much
the same. Perhaps we should view the wickedly effective
weapon of choice, a leather belt with sharp buckle, with a
certain amount of nostalgia. At least it did not cause too much
collateral damage.

*Time has wrought immense changes, Nelson Road and much of Summer Hill has
been demolished and rebuilt several times over the last century.* The Author

Frederick Edward Timbrell was the ringleader of one of the gangs in Edwardian Birmingham. He thought he was a smooth operator, and was nick-named Satin as a result. The trouble was that he lost a certain amount of his smooth exterior in August 1905 when he got into a scrap with William Lacy, a lad from another gang. In the fight Lacy managed to bite off a chunk of his ear. Relations between Satin, Lacy and their respective gangs, not good to start with, turned to open hostility.

At about three on the afternoon of 30 September Arthur Smith and his brother William met up with Satin in Sheepcote Street. Together they went off to the *Robin Hood* pub in Summer Hill Street to meet up with Robert Scott and the rest of the gang. There were over a dozen of them present when Lacy and his friends came in. Lacy and Satin pointedly ignored each other, but the various members of the gangs started fiddling with their belts and knives. Although the gang had been in the pub for over an hour, it seems that few of them had drunk a great deal and they were all reasonably sober. No doubt a rising level of adrenalin kept their heads clear too.

At five-forty Lacy and his gang left the pub, Harry Casey seems to have been the last to leave. They headed off towards Nelson Road. Robert Scott got up and followed Casey outside. He caught up with him at the corner of King Edward Road and they started fighting. Satin and the rest of his gang poured out of the pub and ran up the street to join Scott. Casey, not wanting to be outnumbered, raced off down Nelson Road to catch up with his mates, but Scott caught up with him and the fists and hobnailed boots started flying once again.

The running fight had brought the antagonists into Lacy's home territory. Casey and Scott were fighting right outside Moseley's Horse-dealers where Lacy's brother James worked. Casey was clearly getting the worst of the scrap and managed to duck through the growing mob. He sprinted down the stableyard, blood pouring from several head wounds. Scott tried to follow him but found himself alone, facing Casey threatening to kill him. He backed away and rejoined the crowd outside.

As the two main protagonists left, the mob divided itself into its rival components. Lacy and his friends were heavily outnumbered. Lacy stood in the roadway and pulled a revolver from his pocket, keeping it pointed at the ground.

'I'll shoot you if you don't go away.'

Satin sneered; perhaps he thought he was invulnerable with all his mates around him,

'Then shoot' he replied. It was a pretty stupid thing to say to an enemy with a gun.

Lacy raised the revolver, aimed carefully, and fired a single shot straight into Satin's stomach. Satin collapsed to the ground and the mob started to close in on Lacy. He backed away onto the steps to the Moseley's door, raised the gun again and fired at the mob. It was a misfire; everyone heard the click. Lacy turned and rushed through the door.

Mrs Amelia Moseley was not impressed. She had heard the rumpus outside, and then seen a bunch of thugs fighting on her doorstep and now her stable boy's brother had charged through the door clutching a revolver. She was even less impressed when Casey came into the room with a bloody head, she looked back to see Lacy reloading his gun and flipping the spent cartridge into the ash can. Lacy said the crowd outside would do him in if they caught him. Mrs Amelia Moseley was having none of this.

She picked up a heavy weight and opened the door. Standing at the top of the steps, she faced a milling mob of young men armed with knives, broken bottles and swinging belts.

'I'll knock down the first one that tries to come in.'

She was furious. Very sensibly the mob decided not to storm the house of a lady who could probably wrestle a carthorse to the ground. They wisely decided to disperse.

Satin was in a dreadful state. Groaning in pain Arthur Smith dragged him as far as King Edwards Road where they managed to find him some transport to the Queens Hospital. Inside the house Lacy handed the revolver to his brother, who hid it in a bag of mops. It did not take long for the police to arrive. PC Rollason arrested Lacy and made a brief search for the weapon, but failed to find it. Lacy tried to convince the policeman that he was making a mistake and that he had never seen Satin or the gun or even been out in the street. PC Rollason had heard it all before, Lacy was removed to Kenyon Street Station and charged.

Satin was mortally wounded. The bullet had pierced his lower intestine in no less than seven places, and had also punctured an abdominal artery, carrying pieces of cloth along with it. His father came to see him on the Monday just after he had given his version of the events to the police. There was little that the doctors could do for him and by Thursday, after suffering immense pain, he died.

William Lacy was, not surprisingly, found guilty of murder and sentenced to prison. His brother never handed the revolver over to the police, presumably keeping it just in case the Satin Gang sought revenge.

CHAPTER 24

The Camp Hill Tragedy
1905

Forcing the gun to the base of the skull, he pulled the trigger.

E rnest George Strongitharm was his mother's despair. Born in 1871, he had been given a good education but had then drifted from job to job, settling at nothing. Mostly he worked as an insurance agent since he was literate, but he never seemed to make any money. He scrounged off his sister and mother whenever he could. His mother thought he was basically worthless, a scamp, but still put up with him.

April 1904 found the three of them living at 61 Clarence Road. Mr & Mrs Pearson lived next door with their three children. As the year progressed George was once again penniless, but then he struck on a brilliant wheeze to raise some cash. He sold all the furniture in the house by a deed of sale, regardless of the fact it was not even his. Perhaps he thought the new owner would not have the heart to collect all his family's chattels, but in this he was absolutely wrong. In November Elizabeth Strongitharm saw all her furniture carried out of the house, leaving it virtually

Henry Pearson pleaded with his wife Minnie to return. The Strand Magazine

uninhabitable. She gave up on her son and moved to Manchester. George's sister moved to a house in Ryland Road whilst George himself moved into the Pearson's household as a lodger.

Henry Pearson appears to have had a cool relationship with his wife Minnie. He was a metal worker, specialising in making ship's lanterns. She was thirty-four, the same age as their new lodger, and busy at home all day looking after their children. George, with no proper job to go to, spent plenty of time about the house as well. As the spring of 1905 blossomed, so did the relationship between Minnie and George.

It was not until May that Henry started to suspect that his lodger was cuckolding him. He took him to task about the matter in front of Minnie and the truth came out. Minnie was pregnant with George's child. George was ordered out of the house on 22 May. Minnie swore that she would leave too, unable to be parted from her new lover. That evening Henry gave her a good old fashioned talking to about her duties as a wife and mother. It was not very effective and she was as cold as ice with him.

The next day, normal life appeared to go on as usual until suppertime. Henry sent her out to get the beer to go with their supper. It was only a five-minute trip to the pub to get a jug of ale, but after half an hour Henry decided to go and find out where she had got to. In the next street he found her talking with George; he was furious. They ran off, but he soon caught them.

'If you are a man, then fight me.'

George might have been man enough when it came to bedding Minnie, but he was not going to risk a thrashing from her husband. He pulled out a small cheap revolver and pointed it at Henry. Backing away, Henry saw them turn and walk off down the street. At a discrete distance he followed them to see where on earth they were going. It soon became apparent that George had once again prevailed on his sister's generosity and moved into 6 Ryland Road.

Later that evening Henry and his father went to Ryland Road to plead with Minnie to come home. Minnie and George refused to unlock the door. They stood at the window and Minnie called out to him,

'Never will I live with you again.'

It was the last time Henry saw Minnie alive.

Elizabeth Strongitharm returned from Manchester to see her daughter. Arriving at Ryland Road she was horrified to discover that not only had George insinuated himself back into the house, but he had also brought Minnie Pearson and her three children with him.

'She can't stop here, my son can't keep himself, he's too big a scamp'

George, Minnie and the children had to find somewhere else to live. The trouble was that George had no money and no prospect of earning any. What little cash Minnie had was disappearing fast on food for the children. George was gradually being hemmed in by debts. His temper, never that calm to start with, began to fray and the children were the first to feel his fists.

Using his well practised talent for conning people, George managed to rent a room at 81 Camp Hill on Monday, 3 July. He managed to convince Mr Aston that he had just moved to Birmingham from Manchester and that his furniture was at New Street Station whilst a house was being made ready for them all

Part of the city that has changed dramatically over the last century; Camp Hill was the scene of the murder of Minnie Pearson. John Marks Collection

at Sparkbrook. It was only to be a short term stay and the next Monday George asked for the bill, but then said he needed to stay until Thursday and would settle up with one payment then. He was fast running out of options. On the Thursday morning he obtained a gun licence and bought another revolver from George Bates, the gunmaker of Steelhouse Lane.

The events of the evening Thursday 13 July were to be permanently engraved on the memories of Gladys Pearson. The little girl was only eight, and already having to tend to her baby sister. Although George and the family were supposed to be moving out, he kept making excuses to Mr Aston for delaying. The children were not ready, they were not clean enough, and he went back upstairs.

Gladys was talking to the baby when George came in. Losing his temper, he hit her for making too much noise. Minnie, as any mother would, promptly hit him back. Amid the crying children George pulled out the pistol and hit Minnie in the face with it several times. They wrestled for the gun and, as she tried to get to the door, little Gladys called out,

'Don't shoot Mamma'.

'I will' he shouted.

Forcing the gun to the base of her skull, he pulled the trigger. Dead in an instant, Mamma fell backwards amongst her children.

George was now cornered. Mr Aston was coming up the stairs to find out what the noise was about. George rushed to their suitcase and burst it open, rummaging among the scattered clothes he found his cut-throat razor and slashed at his own neck with it.

Mr Aston found the door chained, but could just see the body of Minnie behind it, surrounded by her hysterical children. He raced off to get a doctor and the police. PC Hadley was quickly on the scene. He put his back to the door and broke open the chain. Inside he found both Minnie and George still alive, though unconscious. Minnie breathed her last just a few seconds after he arrived but George lingered on until the doctor arrived. His clumsy attempt at suicide had resulted in massive blood loss and he expired ten minutes later. The doctor found a note in his pocket.

No doubt people will think this action absurd; but my Wife and I think it best. As regards insanity, we are perfectly sane. We have seen life this past twelve months and enjoyed ourselves A1. Our child, we had great hopes, would have been born in a few days; however circumstances alter. My banking account is overdrawn so we have decided to die together.

Both George and Minnie signed the note, although it seems that Minnie's signature was a forgery. George Strongitharm was held up as a typical example of a moral degenerate in all the public press. His sordid life briefly pilloried in the papers, and then the affair was forgotten.

CHAPTER 25

The Vauxhall Double Murder
1905

He [PC MacAndrew] went upstairs ... to find Maria Purslow lying dead on the bed, with the body of the two-year-old Olivia in her arms.

A century of scientific advance has given us much greater insight into the working of the human mind. A hundred years ago the process had only just started and this dim understanding resulted in some terrible tragedies that hopefully cannot happen today.

Richard Purslow was a twenty-nine-year-old labourer living with his wife Maria and two of his three children at 8 Albion Terrace, off Great Francis Street. Through the summer of 1905 he started to exhibit what appeared to the symptoms of diabetes. He began to suffer serious mood swings, going from maudlin to angry, threatening to kill his wife and children one day, and yet being a loving father and husband the next. Their neighbour, Mary Ann Linforth, could not help noticing that he was 'going funny in the head.' His gradual descent into madness was accelerated when he could no longer go to work at the end of the summer. Without the support of workmates and the regular discipline of work, his world started to close in on him.

Life in the Purslow household became increasingly difficult and Maria asked her sister Ellen Smith if she could look after Richard, their son. Their eldest daughter, Lily, and youngest child, Olivia, remained at home. Richard's threats to kill Maria and the children gradually grew more frequent until by the start of November she realised that some professional help was essential.

Dr Harry Pooler, the district medical officer, saw Richard on 3 November. He diagnosed diabetes and thought that it would be best to recommend an infirmary rather than the asylum. He was uncertain about this and saw Richard again on the 4th. Dr Pooler decided that Richard was seriously ill and should be sent directly to the infirmary. Richard refused to go and so Dr Pooler felt that he had reasonable cause to certify him insane and start the process whereby he could be detained in the asylum. He filled out the necessary forms and sent them to the Parish Relief Officer.

Richard returned from his visit to the doctor in a strange mood. He met Mary Ann in the street. She thought that he was going to be kept in the infirmary and so asked him,

'You've soon come back.'

'Yes' he laughed 'They are going to take me to the asylum. What do you think of it'.

Richard's condition worsened rapidly after this. Through the thin party wall of the houses Mary Ann heard him threatening his wife again and again. Despite this, when he was interviewed by the magistrate on the 7th, he appeared rational and normal. The magistrate therefore decided that Dr Pooler did not have sufficient cause to have Richard locked away in the asylum. Since the law required both doctor and magistrate to agree, Richard was allowed to go home.

Richard seemed comparatively lucid on Saturday the 18th. During the afternoon he had spoken briefly with Mary Ann, telling her that his illness was getting more painful and he feared he was dying. He was drinking beer in the *Train Tavern* in the evening, but not to any excess. Maria came in at about eleven and he asked for some whiskey to take home. The barman sold him a quarter bottle rather than the pint that he asked for, not because he

Maria and Olivia Purslow were doomed by Frank's madness. The Strand Magazine

was drunk but because the barman knew that he was unwell. Richard and Maria walked quietly down Albion Terrace, bidding a polite Good Night to their neighbour Harriet Hadley. The terrace settled down for the night.

At four in the morning Mary Ann's husband woke her up. Down in the yard Richard was pacing around anxiously, hooting and crying 'I am mad.... Do get up ...' Mary rapped on the party wall, expecting to hear a reply from Maria, but there was only silence. She hurried down to the yard to find Richard waving a kitchen knife about and clearly very distressed.

'Mr Purslow, what are you doing out here on a cold night like this' she tried to calm him and managed to get the knife out of his hand. Leading him into his kitchen she banked up the fire. He kept repeating 'I've drunk poison.'

'Oh such nonsense' said Mary Ann. Finally he said,

'I have done it. She is dead. I have murdered my wife and the little Ciss.'

Turning to the stairs he opened the door and said

'Come and see, I'll show you what I have done.'

Mary Ann decided this was too much; she went round to the Hadley's house and asked Mr Hadley to get the police. They had already been woken by the commotion. Alfred Hadley managed to find PC MacAndrew on his beat and returned with him. He went upstairs to the bedroom to find Maria Purslow lying dead on the bed, with the body of the two-year-old Olivia in her arms. Maria had been strangled and the baby suffocated with a pillow. Lily, the oldest daughter, had slept through it all, but now she woke up and started to scream.

Downstairs, the increasingly hysterical Richard was clutching his throat and continued to say he had drunk poison. PC MacAndrew forced him to drink salt water until he was sick. He had drunk a lineament containing ammonia, but not enough to seriously harm him. He was arrested and taken to Bloomsbury Street Station. There he was charged with causing the death of his wife and child as well as trying to commit suicide.

Richard Purslow was in no fit state to attend trial. His mind rapidly disintegrated and he was remanded to an asylum. Although the doctor had seen the danger signs, the magistrate had not, seeing Richard on what they all agreed later, was one of his last Good Days.

CHAPTER 26

The Murder of 'Birmingham Lizzie'
1913
Rushing back inside, they found Lizzie on the floor, her dress blazing with burning paraffin.

irmingham Lizzie' had quite a reputation. She was once known as Mrs Emily Davies, but had left her soldier husband in 1903 and embarked on a life that was later described as dissolute and drunken. She left Birmingham for the bright lights of London and plied her business at the *Albion* pub, Kings Cross. She kept in touch with the West family who lived at 115 Bissell Street.

Edith Mumford travelled to London to fetch Birmingham Lizzie. The Strand Magazine

Edith Mumford, the daughter of the Wests, knew a painter by the name of Frank Greening, nick named 'Mad Frank'. He sent her a note to ask her if she would take a letter to Birmingham Lizzie, by now called Elizabeth Ellen Hearne. The note was to ask her to come and live with him. Presumably they were already acquainted. Edith and Lizzie agreed to return by train to Birmingham.

They arrived back at New Street on 16 February and the next day Lizzie and Frank rented rooms off Mrs West at 52 Rea Street South. Edith moved into one of her mother's houses at 21 Ashley Street. The Rea Street tenement was not particularly wholesome; with the river Rea right behind them and so on 4 March they moved to Gooch Street. A fortnight later they moved yet again; to Claybrook Street. Their relationship was anything but idyllic, with Lizzie's drunkenness and Mad Frank's tendency towards sudden outbursts of violence, their quarrels could be heard across the street.

A hint of the storm to come happened at a party at Edith's house in Ashley Street on 26 March. Annie West and her daughter had stepped outside for a private chat when they heard a crash. Rushing back inside, they found Lizzie on the floor, her dress blazing with burning paraffin. Mrs West managed to put the flames out and accused Frank of throwing a lamp at her. Frank denied it, saying that it had merely got knocked over. Later that night Lizzie told Annie that he had indeed thrown it, but somehow they patched things up and the couple went home to Claybrook Street in peace. It was not destined to last long.

Frank did not really help pacify things when, on 31st March, he invited Rose Butler and Kate Cowley to come and live with them at Claybrook Street. His ardour for the quarrelsome Lizzie was clearly fading. On the evening of 2 April they had yet another massive row, partly about Lizzie's visits to Edith's house, which by now had gained the reputation of being full of loose women. This row escalated into a fight and Frank only quietened Lizzie down by banging her on the head with a lamp. The next morning he asked Rose if she wanted to come and live with him in Wolverhampton or Coventry. Since this

Like Bissell Street, Rea Street has undergone a transformation. In particular the River Rea has been cleaned up and is no longer a vast open sewer poisoning everyone living around it. It is culverted to the right of the street. The Author

was in front of Lizzie it was hardly the most tactful way of hinting at the end of their tempestuous relationship. Lizzie just shrugged and said 'Do not take notice of him, he's mad'

A couple of days later Lizzie had drunk herself into such a stupor that she was arrested and fined. Frank paid the fine. Lizzie poured out her troubles to Mrs West, showing her the wound on her head and telling her that she was now sleeping in the attic rather than with Frank. The coterie of girls at Claybrook Street and Bissell Street all took her side in the affair.

Frank meanwhile was muttering dark threats about doing away with Lizzie. He was not alone either. He kept in contact with his mother and Mr & Mrs Garratly as well as a friend

Thomas Wood. He told the Garratlys about how Lizzie was constantly drunk and always quarrelling. He was frequently upset about Lizzie going to the house in Ashley Street. What he hadn't told them was that in early March he had bought a revolver. Lizzie had found this and hidden it in the cellar.

On Sunday 6 April their relationship was definitely over. At about ten in the morning Rose Butler came downstairs to find Lizzie cleaning the grate. Frank was standing close by and commented that Lizzie would not need to do that again. A couple of hours passed in the tense household until at noon Mrs West arrived to collect the rent. Business done, Lizzie and Frank went to the nearby pub with Mrs West. Edith and Mr West joined them. Frank needed to collect his clothes and things from the house. Mr West had a set of keys so the two of them left the girls in the pub and returned to the house. Frank gathered up a few of his clothes and, it appears, found the revolver in the cellar. He hurriedly scrawled a note on a postcard for Mr West to give to Lizzie. It read:

> You can do your worst, and we will see you win, you should see what your friends might do for you now.' Much of the note was illegible, but it ended 'serving them other girls a dirty trick.

The note shows Frank's excited and nervous mood, and also hints that his relationship with Rose has become established. Frank left Mr West and went to his friends, Mr & Mrs Garratly. Mr West got back to the pub and gave the note to Lizzie; she didn't seem bothered about it in the least. Mr & Mrs West went home and after a few more drinks Lizzie and Edith went to Ida Bolding's house in the courtyard at the back of 115 Bissell Street. There Ida was cooking lunch, Lizzie sat on the sofa and Edith was standing up when Frank suddenly burst in.

'Give me the key'.

'I haven't got it, the landlady has got it.'

'Rose is waiting in the street for her clothes; she can't wait there all day, I want my clothes.'

'You never had any clothes..... I don't care for the shooter you have got.'

'Woman you must be mad, I haven't got such a thing'

But he had, and had just pulled it out of his pocket too. He held it behind his back and checked that there was no one in the courtyard, turned back and fired three shots at Lizzie, every one striking her. Edith screamed and he turned and fired a shot at her. It grazed her eyebrow and buried itself in the plaster. Frank turned up his collar and hurried off across the yard.

Lizzie lay on the sofa, one bullet had gone right through her thigh, the other two into her chest. Edith and Ida called for help in getting her to the hospital.

Frank hurried round to his friends the Garratly's. He was almost laughing as he told Mrs Garratly: 'Lizzie's met with an accident; in fact I've shot her, and this is what I did it with' he indicated the gun in his pocket. He seems to have been partly hysterical and made his way to the hospital where he sat for a while with Lizzie. He left when Mrs West arrived. 'It was him' Lizzie said when Mrs West asked who had done such a thing.

Frank wandered back to Claybrook Street, where Detective Constable Jones spotted him. Taking no chances, Jones ordered him to put up his hands, indicating that he too was

The only buildings left from the time of Birmingham Lizzie are the pubs. 115 is just a workshop, but the pub where she drank is still there. The Author

armed. Frank didn't resist arrest. During his long night in the cells, Lizzie died from her wounds. Frank was now on a charge of wilful murder.

There was little he could muster in his defence apart from the constant quarrels and provocation that he had suffered. None of this was considered sufficient reason to shoot his woman. He was sentenced to death on 14 July and on 13 August the new hangman, Pierrepoint, carried out the sentence at Warwick Gaol.

CHAPTER 27

The Winson Green Canal Murder
1927
They hauled the body of the young woman out of the dark water.

The canal towpath at Winson Green was a quiet and secluded place. The first canal to Birmingham took a very roundabout route to the city, following a single level. Years later the route was straightened and this left lots of loops to each side of the New Main Line. The loops were still fairly busy with boats but nothing like the vast numbers that hauled coal up and down the main line. Winson Green was turned into an island when the new line was cut and the old canal towpath became a pleasant walk for courting couples. It was the property of the Birmingham Canal Navigation Company, which meant that anyone on it was trespassing. This made little difference to the amount of couples walking along it on a quiet summers evening with little more in mind than a peaceful cuddle out of the sight of various parents and gossips.

Olive Gordon Turner was walking with her sweetheart, Charles Broomhead, along the old canal on the evening of 2 July 1927. They were not the only couple about at 11 that night. In the fast fading daylight, the landscape was still lit by the fires of the various forges and foundries backing onto the canal, Doris Emery and Edgar Willock were exchanging sweet nothings on their walk too.

Olive and Charles had known each other for nigh on nine months and had been walking out together for the last three. Olive came from Ford Street and Charles was from Devonshire Street, both in Hockley. Olive's sister, Ivy, was walking out with Charles's best friend James Rooke. Both Olive and Ivy lived with their grandmother because their parents had died. This Saturday night Olive and Charles

The scene of the murder, the girl was dragged here, knocked unconscious and flung in the canal. Her boyfriend, Charles, lay unconscious on the towpath. The Author

decided to treat themselves to a trip to the picture house at Winson Green. The film ended at about ten-fifteen and they took the scenic route home along the towpath of the Old Canal.

They were about twenty yards from the arm of the canal leading to Lodge Road when they saw a tall man approaching them from Clissold Street direction. He had an upright stature and was wearing a dark grey suit with a somewhat dirty collar and twisted tie. He was clean-shaven and spoke with authority,

'You are trespassing up here.'

The young couple, Olive was only eighteen, were intimidated by his manner and thought he was a policeman. He asked them for their names and addresses. Charles had no way of proving his identity and the man said,

'I shall have to take you in then.'

Charles noticed with some concern that the man produced no notebook to record their names. At the man's command, they followed him back along the canal towards Winson Green. After a short while they passed two more couples leaning against the asylum wall.

'Why don't you move these, they are standing.'

'I've got two, and that's enough for me'.

The man stopped talking as they passed the first couple. Thomas Hill noticed the tall man distinctly but took little notice of the younger man. The Canal Company was renowned for doing anything to get money, charging high tolls for freight, extortionate rates for cooling water, and especially fining people for trespassing. The appearance of someone looking like a detective on the towpath was worrying and distinctive.

As they passed the second couple the man turned to them and said,

'You know you can square me, but it is up to yourself.'

Charles answered,

'No, you take me, let the girl go home, she's got no mother or father and her grandmother is waiting for her.'

'No' the man replied, ' I'll take the two.'

Charles realised that he would have to bribe the man rather than face charges of trespass. He only had four pence left after his night at the pictures, but he offered it anyway.

'No, fourpence is no good to me.' he sneered.

Olive opened her bag and offered to find some money, but Charles told her not to.

It was now that Edgar Willock and his sweetheart Doris walked past them. Edgar distinctly heard the mention of money. They were walking back from Winson Green too after spending the evening at Bordesley Green Picture House. They passed Charles, Olive and the stranger near the bridge over the arm of the canal to Hockley Canal Basins and Lodge Road.

Doris turned to Edgar and said 'Stop a little, I think there is something up with those three.'

Charles, Olive and the tall man continued walking towards Winson Green. Charles was getting deeply suspicious of this tall stranger who seemed to be a detective but wanted a bribe. He turned to Olive and told her to run for it. She needed no further encouragement and flew back down the towpath as fast as she could go. The man took a couple of moments to realise what had happened, sprinted after her, and Charles then ran after him. Pounding down the towpath Charles managed to catch up with the stranger and grabbed his jacket. The stranger stopped, turned and grabbed his waistcoat, then smashed his fist into the side of Charles's face. Charles dropped to the ground completely stunned. The man continued his chase of Olive.

Skirts flying, Olive raced down the towpath until she caught up with Edgar and Doris.

Western Road Bridge. It was just here that the murderer caught up with Olive, Doris and Edgar. He dragged Olive back under the bridge to her doom. The Author

'There is a fellow up there who says he is a policeman. He is after you as well as me. Run with me' She caught Doris by the hand and they started running.

They got as far as Western Road Bridge before the tall man caught up with them. Olive was half fainting with exhaustion and Edgar propped her up as she swooned at the sight of the stranger. He put his arm between Edgar and Doris, then grabbed both girls by the wrists.

'Come on'. said the man.

'Who are you? What are you up to?' asked Edgar.

'I am a police officer.' The man replied with such authority that both Edgar and Doris believed him. He caught hold of Olive by the waist and glowered at Edgar and Doris.

'Don't interfere' said Doris, 'it is nothing to do with you. He is a police officer.'

They turned back and hurriedly left the scene. Soon afterwards they met another couple and warned them away.

Back on the towpath near the canal arm bridge, Charles staggered to his feet. Regaining his wits, he realised he was alone. There was no sign of Olive, the stranger or the other couples. He ran up to the bridge to try to see anyone. There was just one man, wearing a trilby hat, coming down from Winson Green. Charles explained what had happened, and in the meantime another man, Mr Bird, joined them, as did another. They walked up the canal arm but found no one.

Edgar and Doris ran towards Winson Green, finally finding a policeman in Aberdeen Street.

'Come with me to the canal' gasped Edgar, but the policeman had other business,

'I will be round there in about half an hour, I'll see then.'

Despairing of assistance from the officer they found a man on a bicycle by Winson Green Road Bridge. He, too, was searching,

'Have you seen a woman round this way? Because she was going to do herself in.'

Edgar told him about the incident by Western Road Bridge.

'Was she well dressed?'

'She was' replied Edgar

'That is not her, I am looking for a married woman with a large family, who has threatened to drown herself.'

'Come down with me' answered Edgar 'and see if we can see the woman.'

They walked Doris home and then the two of them returned to the canal and walked as far as the bridge on the canal arm. There was no one in sight at all. Edgar went home.

Charles decided to find his friend James Rooke for help. James and Ivy had been to the Reservoir Dance Hall but had returned to their homes at ten. Charles called in at Olive's home on his way to get James. Ivy was asleep in bed but her grandmother woke her up and told her what was going on. Charles and James returned to the canal to search some more.

Ivy got dressed and went around to James's house to wait for their return. The midnight hours ticked slowly by. At quarter past one they returned but with no news of what had happened to Olive. They went out once more determined to find her and to get the police. This time they took a flare with them and by its flickering light they found Olive's hat, bag and fur lying on the towpath beside the wall on Lodge Road Arm. They carried them back to James's house.

At first light the police started to drag the canal where Olive's bag was found. Only a few yards away the dragline caught hold of something. They hauled the body of the young woman out of the dark water. She was still fully clothed and had not been molested in any way, simply hit on the head and thrown in the canal to drown. Her watch had stopped at eleven forty-one.

The hunt was on for the tall man who impersonated a policeman; he had some serious questions to answer. The number of clear and accurate descriptions gave the police enough to work with. It appears that they had someone in mind almost straight away.

On 6 July they took Charles to a factory in Smethwick to watch the people coming out, but he failed to recognise any of them. Later that day they then took him to Cannings Factory in Kenyon Street. After watching the stream of workers emerging from the factory gate, he suddenly recognised the man. Sergeant Edwards who was near Charles, chased the man and arrested him. Over the next couple of days most of the direct witnesses were asked to attend an identification parade. Almost all of them picked this man out, either individually or with another who looked very similar.

James Joseph Power went on trial in December 1927. He had indeed once been a policeman, but one that turned bad. He had been run out of the force a fair while before and was already accused of committing a rape on another woman. The confident identification by so many witnesses ensured that he was found guilty. Powers himself maintained his innocence until the last. He insisted that a jealous police superintendent had framed him. His pleas fell on deaf ears and the Judge had no compunction about sentencing him to the gallows. Months of appeals managed to get this reduced to life imprisonment.

CHAPTER 28

Dark days on the Birmingham Canal

... her bedraggled body was dragged from the water, a photo of Harry tucked in her clothes.

The Birmingham Canal Navigation is at the very heart of the nation's waterways. At the start of the twentieth century it was at it's very peak. Whilst other canals suffered from railway competition, the BCN took freight from the trains and moved it to the very wharves of the factories. Millions of tons of cargo on Joeys and Joshers cruised through the city. Waterways history is full of statistics around this topic and yet remains strangely silent on the other side of the story, the relationship of the city to the canal. It is not a pretty one, it has no roses or castles. It is the story of the unrelenting pressure of the Industrial Revolution on an urban society and the canal was often the place where the pressure blew. The story can be found in the coroner's reports.

The Birmingham Coroner had the unpleasant task of determining the cause of death in cases where there was any doubt. His district contained only a fraction of the Birmingham canals, from Camp Hill Locks in the east to Smethwick in the west, Aston Locks in the north to the Worcester & Birmingham Canal in the south. It was a seething metropolis and behind the fame of manufacturing and industry lay a vast well of poverty and crime. People pushed by exhaustion, working twelve hour, six day weeks, pushed by hunger from the miserable wages, by gossip, jealousy and gin.

Emily Hicks was just seventeen in September 1892. Her story is by no means unusual. She had recently recovered from a rheumatic fever, well enough to spend a Thursday night with her friend, Ellie, at the Steam Clock Music Hall. Returning home rather late she rowed with her mother, who said she would break her neck if she went there again and that people who went to such places deserved to be put in the cut. The next day Emily's mother returned from work at ten in the evening to find a note.

> *Dear Mother, I have gone to do what you wish me, give my love to my brothers and sisters and their two little ones. It is a shame to destroy my young life so soon. Don't let this trouble you.*

Whilst her mother had been at work Emily had met Ellie and seemed very upset about the row, but apparently recovered. Emily met up with Ellie later that afternoon with even worse news. She had discovered her boyfriend Harry Hayling was walking out with another girl. Emily wrote a last note to Harry for Ellie to deliver and was last seen walking towards the canal. The next day her bedraggled body was dragged from the water, a photo of Harry tucked in her clothes.

The canal was dragged pretty often in those days. It was on 18th April 1895, but with a rather strange twist. The day

Farmers Bridge was a secluded place used by gangs and criminals. The Author

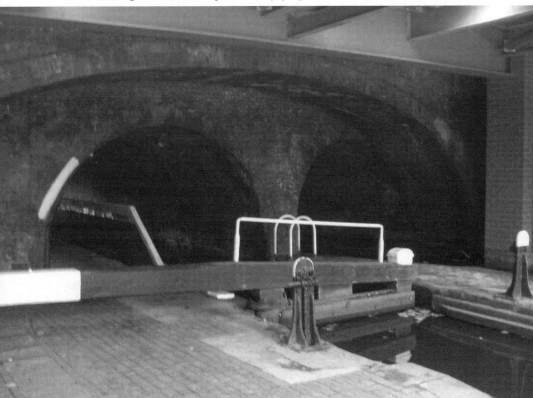

before Rose Foster had left her mothers house to return to her aunts. She really did not like living with her aunt, Harriett, at the *George Inn*, Smethwick; indeed she had told a friend that she would rather drown, but she could not stay with her mother. She was only thirteen, so no one paid any attention to her. Thomas Taplar saw Rose from his boat; she was sheltering under a bridge during a thunderstorm. Some boys on another boat claimed to have heard a scream and a splash but they didn't bother to investigate. Rose's mother returned home to find the girl gone and raised the alarm. There was little that could be done overnight. The next morning the police started to drag the canal beneath Spring Hill Bridge.

During the night, Harriett had had a frightful dream. She was walking along the canal and brushed the tip of her umbrella in the water, beneath the ripples she suddenly saw Rose looking up at her. Awake, she rushed down to the cut and persuaded the police to move their dragline down the canal to Blews Street, the place she remembered from her dream. Within minutes they pulled out the girl's corpse.

The boatmen were used to all this. Drowning oneself in the canal was a common way to commit suicide, particularly for women. Of the ten women who committed suicide in 1897, five drowned themselves whilst the rest used poison, hanging or cut their throats. That year twenty-eight men did away with themselves, not one of them by drowning. The statistics belie the true numbers since unless there was very clear evidence for suicide the coroner would record an accidental death. Turning up a corpse was seriously awkward for a boatman since he would be forced to delay his journey whilst the police enquiries were under way. Richard Hetherington, the Canal Policeman at Selly Oak was not surprised to receive an unsigned note, 'There is a man floating opposite Somerset Road Station in the canal. I think it is time he was got out. You will find him there.' Henry Jackson had been in there at least ten days.

Often the boatmen were the first on the scene. William Harrad had been drinking with his friends in the *Horse and Jockey*. They wanted to know if his dog could swim, so a little later he chucked it in the canal. Half an hour later a boatman

Approaching the city along the Worcester & Birmingham Canal, today, the place looks very civilised, but a century ago the body of Henry Jackson floated here for days before anyone pulled him out. The Author

pointed out his body to a passer by but did not stop. It was presumed that William fell in. Arthur Wilkes had already rescued the dog. This attitude of indifference by the boatmen did not enhance their image. When George Bradshaw went swimming in the cut at Selly Oak, and promptly drowned, a passing boat refused to stop or even lend a boat hook to help get his corpse out. George was just one of the dozens of children who discovered the hard way that canals really are dangerous. One of the jury described the boatman as inhuman, although the coroner merely stated that, in his experience, the boatmen rarely stopped to render assistance for fear of being called to the inquest.

The canal staff were constantly involved in recovering bodies, although in one case in a rather unorthodox way. Ashted Locks were drained for cleaning in May 1904, and the workmen discovered a skeleton in the mud. A young toll clerk gathered the bones up, washed them and took them down the pub. Everyone thought this was great fun, apart from the lad's mum, who was not having them in the house. She called the police who took them to a distinctly unimpressed coroner. The remains were never identified.

Working on the canal could be dangerous. On 13 March 1901, Earnest Ricketts and his mate King were bringing their boat along the canal by Somerset Road station. Ahead of them, going in the same direction was another boat fully laden with slack coal. The horse pulling the laden boat was on its own, the crew being in the boat cabin. Earnest called 'whoa' and the laden horse stopped. The towrope slackened and dropped to the ground so that Earnest's unladen boat could float over the rope and his horse step over it. Overtaking with horse drawn boats is a bit complicated and needs well-behaved

The Birmingham & Fazeley Canal ran right through the heart of one of the poorest parts of the city. It was the scene of many suicides. The Author

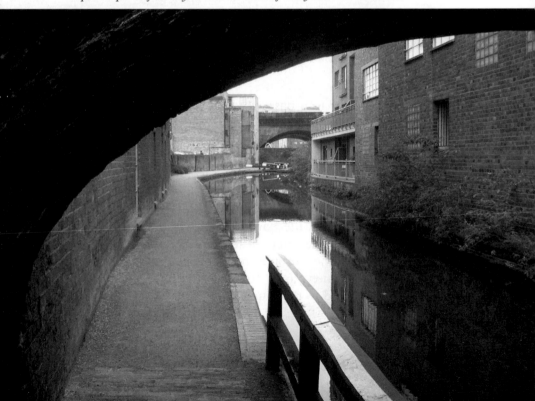

animals. Earnest's horse was anything but, it had bolted three times one day and now, just as it stepped over the towrope, it reared up and bolted again. The rope to Earnest's boat broke and whipped about his waist and neck. The horse galloped up the path, dragging him along the dirt and into the cut. King leapt off the boat and eventually caught the horse. It was too late for Earnest; he had been killed.

Edward Walters was only fourteen in December 1892, but he was already working hard on his father's boat. He slipped on the icy cabin roof and fell in the canal. Unable to swim in the freezing water he was drowned, leaving his distraught father to pull him out with a boat hook. Life on the boats was unrelentingly hard and often brief.

Local boatmen had homes on the bank and could spend the day working the boats in and around Birmingham and the Black Country. The canal system extended right the way across England and there was another class of boatmen who lived on their boats.

These boatmen lived in a very different and isolated world with its own set of rules. Whole families lived and died within the cramped confines of their cabins, usually measuring about 8′ long, 7′ wide and only 5′ high. They had been reduced from once proud and industrious hauliers to complete poverty and destitution by the railways. They tended to be shunned by the rural communities they passed through because it was thought that they carried diseases from the cities. They were shunned in the cities because it was thought they would swipe anything that was not nailed down. A gross slander if ever there was one, you would need to weld it down.

On Thursday 5 March 1908 John Ward moored his boat up beside two others at the Fazeley Street wharf and wandered into the *Vulcan Inn* for a couple of pints at eleven. He went back to his boat in the afternoon and returned for another half pint at about six. Apparently he then left hurriedly and that was the last anyone saw of him alive.

His boat stayed moored up, unattended and generally in everyone's way until Sunday. That was the day that they fished his body out of the canal. It soon transpired that John Ward had not simply fallen, someone had given him a massive blow

This flight of locks in the city centre was renowned for the amount of still born babies dumped into its dark waters. The Author

to the side of the head which had killed him stone dead long before he hit the water. This, however, was the canal system; the jury returned an open verdict and let the matter drop.

The canals of Birmingham were almost all owned by the Birmingham Canal Navigations Ltd. The company had been trading since the eighteenth century and had developed a reputation for being avaricious and ruthless. They kept the locks and towpaths in good order, but saw no reason to waste good money on things like fences to keep children away from the water. They were supposed by law, but somehow never quite seemed to get around to it. The city councillors were forever asking the company to fence off and gate the exposed parts of the canal like Fazeley Street Bridge, but it never happened and the toll of suicides continued to rise. One of the most distressing was the demise of Emma Stewart. She had a mental breakdown on 5 April 1898. She had apparently been happily enough in her marriage to the brass polisher William Edward Stewart. They lived in one of the little courtyards off Holt Street and had two little girls, Lily May, who was nearly three and Emma Jemima who was just sixteen months. Emma Stewart muttered something about there being a whole lot of trouble brewing for them before she walked down to Fazeley Street Bridge, tied Lily May to her apron strings, held tightly onto Emma and threw herself in.

Crowds gathered whilst the police dragged the canal all afternoon. They soon found the mother and oldest child, but it was not until the next day, when they moved one of the barges and the baby floated briefly to the surface. A brave young man named Albert Stratton dived into the canal and grabbed the little corpse before it sank out of sight. The open gate to the canal seemed to be a terrible temptation to seek the solace of a Lethean sleep.

It was not just the Birmingham Company that was hopeless at fencing. Sandy Lane on the Warwick and Birmingham was another black spot. Tempers flared when Amelia Newbold went and threw herself in the canal there. She was part hysterical and very depressed, there was no gate or fence and after asking a stranger where the cut was, her last words were 'See me make a hole in it'. The coroner had repeatedly asked the Warwick Company to fence that exact place after several children had drowned there.

Only once did the coroner have to deal with something unrelated to human misery and death, and it came as quite a shock. He had to call for advice on a case of treasure trove.

Today this quiet residential mooring gives no hint of the huge quantities of goods that were moved day & night from boats to trains and wagons for delivery around the city. This area of canal features many times in the annals of Birmingham crime. The Author

Albert Ingram, a schoolboy of fourteen, was collecting dandelion leaves for his pet rabbit on the embankment by Winson Green Bridge, when he slipped. As he slithered to a halt he dislodged the turf and found a matted pile of twenty sovereigns and other coins in the remnants of a metal box. The coins all dated from before 1887. Isaac Bradley, the coroner, declared them to be treasure trove. It was an interesting day, but then back to the remorseless grind of drowned distressed damsels, battered boatmen and the occasional murder.

CHAPTER 29

The Aston Mystery
1929

It was clear that there was rather a lot more to her death than met the eye.

In a world before complicated forensic science, the city coroner occasionally had his work really cut out for him. Luckily, even in 1929, the city was still small enough for gossip and a casual glance to be crucial to the unravelling of a complex mystery.

Sarah Elizabeth Astley, the fifty-nine-year-old widow of a canal boatman was found dead on her bed on 24 August. She lived at 9, Laburnum Grove, Pugh Road, Aston, which was a small community in which little passed unnoticed. This was to be a great help to the investigation although not decisive.

The real problem was that Mrs Astley seemed to have shot herself some time after she had died. In the general way of things this seemed a little odd, to put it mildly. Chief Detective Superintendent Burnett was instructed by the coroner to find out what on earth had happened.

Simply put, Mrs Astley appeared to have written a suicide note and then shot herself in the neck with a small .22 calibre pistol that she held in her left hand. All very neat and tidy, but for several objections that were immediately raised. She was right-handed, had not the faintest idea about how to use a gun, was not in the least bit suicidal and, crucially, her heart had stopped beating several minutes before the shot was fired. It was clear that there was rather a lot more to her death than met the eye. Someone had tried to make it look like suicide, although the motive for doing this to a lady who was already dead of natural causes was a conumdrum.

The puzzle opened on the morning of Saturday 24 August. Noticing that Sarah's door was ajar and the curtains still drawn, Mrs Hutt, one of her neighbours, went in to see if everything was all right. On the living room table she found a note:

> *Poll*
> *i in teribel pain my head shal go mad ; I sure ospital said all time getting worce,*
> *Come*

Although the irregular spelling of the note was typical of a partially literate canal worker, the handwriting did not resemble that of Sarah when compared to other things she had written.

Upstairs, the neighbour found Sarah lying on top of the bed, wearing only some of her underwear. There was a pistol in her left hand and a small bullet wound in her neck just below her ear. There was no blood on the bed, or anywhere else in the house. There were a couple of bruises on her lips, but no other signs of violence. By now the other neighbours in the street were aware something was amiss. PC Swift was called in and surveyed the scene. Unfortunately he moved the gun so that further analysis of its position could not be carried out. The gunshot wound was not surrounded by any singeing of hair; so the gun must have been at least nine inches away when fired. Sarah's corpse was removed to the mortuary.

Sarah's daughter, Florence Gertrude Lees, came to identify the body. She swore that her mother was right handed, and that the handwriting of the note was not hers. She also stated that her mother had never owned a gun and would not have had the slightest idea of how to use one. The gun itself was a rather smart little .22 calibre revolver with an inlaid ivory handle. It was well polished by regular handling and contained five live and one spent cartridge. These were short shot type and reasonably easy to trace.

The police started to question the residents of Laburnum Grove about the previous evening. Mrs Sarah Astley was a quiet neighbour who mostly kept to herself. She was very deaf, but slim and sprightly for her age. She usually bought herself a pint of ale from the off-licence at the corner of Pugh Road and Sycamore Road before retiring to bed at about nine. If she did have visitors she would buy a quart or more, although this was rare. She worked for Messrs Berry's at the Sand Pitts. Like virtually all the other houses in the Grove, her house was rented from an agency.

The evening of the 23rd was the key to unravelling the mystery. In this the residents of Laburnum Grove had plenty of conflicting clues for the detectives. Frank Barber at the off-licence said that Sarah had come in at about eight fifty-five in a very good mood, very jolly, and had bought a quart of ale. This in itself was unusual since she tended to be tactiturn. Mary Brockington of No 6 saw Sarah going off to get the beer, and significantly she also saw a man come out of the house shortly afterwards. He went to the public lavatories. She did not catch a glimpse of his face, but he was about 5'7" tall, with round shoulders. She noticed later that the living room gas light was on at ten forty-five, which was very unusual. At ten fifty-five she heard a loud noise like some one hitting a tin. Alice Barber, the wife of Frank at the off licence, swore that she heard a shot ring out at nine forty-five. There were fireworks going off at the same time but the sound came from another direction. She was in the yard at the time with her eight year old nephew who asked 'Was it a shot Auntie?' She was convinced it was a gunshot similar to those she had heard when she was growing up in the country, and it came from the direction of Laburnum Grove. She didn't think much about it until the furore the next day.

Gladys Maud Brazier lived directly opposite Sarah Astley's house. She arrived back from work at ten twenty-five and noticed that the lights were on both upstairs and down. This was very unusual, and so was the way that the bedroom curtains were drawn. They were pinned together in the middle. Normally if Mrs Astley wanted a little extra privacy she stuck a bit of paper in the gap in the middle. Gladys went out a little later to post a letter. On her way back at ten fifty-five she saw a fellow coming out of Sarah's garden gate; closing the gate with his right hand and reaching for a bicycle with his left. She didn't catch sight of his face but noticed he had dark curly hair and was of a slim build and medium height. He pushed the bike out of the Grove. Gladys noticed that the

living room light was now out but the bedroom one was still
on. Her lodger noticed that it was still on at two-thirty.

Mr & Mrs Hutt were walking down the Grove at about
eleven and noticed the cyclist too. Mr Hutt thought that he
was bareheaded, but with his collar turned up and face turned
away from them, whilst Mrs Hutt thought he was wearing a
Trilby.

The hunt was on for this unknown cyclist and the other man
who had been seen earlier.

The police turned to Sarah Astley's employer to see if there
was anything to be gleaned there. Marion Greene, the
manageress, could not provide any information directly
relating to the incident, but gave the police a valuable lead to
follow up. Sarah had had a relationship with the rent collector
some time ago. The other residents of the Grove soon backed
this up. He used to call at Sarah's for the rent rather more
often than the rent was due, several times a week at one point.

The police called at the office. Although the rent officer in
question no longer worked for the company, there was little
doubt in their mind just who was in question: Howard Benson
of Kings Heath.

*The tram terminus at Kings Heath was where Howard Benson collected Sarah
and others for some 'private entertainment' whilst his wife was on holiday.* John
Marks Collection

A somewhat sordid story began to emerge as the police interviewed Sarah's employer, her friends and the people at the estate agents. A dozen years before, Sarah had lost her husband and she was left in comparative poverty. Eventually she struck up a relationship with the rent collector. Sexual favours as a way of paying the rent were not entirely unheard of, although this relationship seems to have lasted quite some time. Benson, however, managed to get himself the sack from his original estate agency firm because his exploitation of the poorer tenants became too well known. He took a new position with a firm based in Temple Street some four years before this dark event. He maintained contact with Sarah by persuading her to visit him at his new office, quite possibly helping her find the money for the new rent collector. The liaison was common knowledge at Sarah's workplace. She used to finish early on Saturdays, and sometimes Fridays too, just to see her man.

One time, roughly two years before, Sarah, together with another woman and man, went to Kings Heath and were seen drinking in a pub there. It was whilst Benson's wife was on holiday. Sarah confided all the details to her close friend, Mary Ann Bradburn. The details included not only the sessions in the office and at Kings Heath, but also the identity of one of the several other women that Benson was seeing. She even pointed out one young widow in the street. She had been servicing Bensons desires since the previous August Bank Holiday. Sarah met this widow just as she and Benson were coming out of his office one Saturday afternoon. They started laughing at Sarah, much to her indignation. 'Don't you laugh at me you brazen hussy' she shouted before giving Benson a real talking to and threatened to tell his wife.

A couple of weeks after Easter, Mary Bradburn visited Sarah in response to a very distressed letter. When she got to Laburnum Grove Sarah told her that Benson had given her venereal disease. She was incandescent with fury, although there seemed little she could do about it. Marion Greene at work refused to write a letter to Benson's wife revealing the extent of her husband's infidelity on the grounds that she would not make another woman's life any worse. Sarah thought about approaching the wife herself, and went to the office to confront Benson with the prospect. Benson was furious; even if he had always insisted to Sarah that he had no real love of his wife; she had a brother who had already given him a thrashing for misbehaving. They made up and he gave her a shilling.

Sarah was not mollycoddled for long and her feelings of exploitation soon resurfaced. Quite possibly the arrival of the much younger widow on the scene aggravated matters, as well as the infection. On 10 August she spent a fair while in a pub and then waited for three hours outside Benson's office. She then discovered that Mrs Benson was on holiday and he was at home in Taylor Road. She went to the house in Kings Heath and discovered the young widow there. A shouting match ensued.

Benson was leaving a trail of embittered women behind him. On 14 August a girl and child appeared at the office whilst he was out, and left a letter for him. Sarah was back at the office on Friday, the 16th. Alice Smith, the office cleaner heard an almighty row break out in Benson's office. She distinctly heard chairs being thrown about and shouting. It ended with Benson yelling 'Get out of it, will you' three times. The door slammed and Alice looked down the stairwell to see Sarah leaving the building.

Sarah was still furious the next day. She visited the office once again; she caught him by the collar:

'I will strangle you, you dirty dog. I will give you giving it to me. Why don't you give it to someone else.'

She hit him until he threatened to call the police in. By now everyone in the office, if not Temple Street, knew what was going on. Sarah stormed out.

The police decided that an interview with Mr Howard Benson would be very helpful. Chief Inspector H Hawkins of the Coroner's Office called round to the Temple Street Office on 26 August. Benson admitted only to knowing Sarah as a tenant from some time past. He absolutely denied that she had been to his house in the past, and when pressed came up with some story about Sarah being in Kings Heath to visit her employer. Benson said that it would be more than his job was worth to have anything more to do with the tenants than simply collect the rent. The Inspector noticed a bicycle in the office and asked Benson if it was his. Benson admitted it was, but said he had never visited Mrs Astley. He then went on to tell the Inspector that, on the night in question, he had been at home for a time, before taking a long bicycle ride alone. He returned home at eleven-thirty.

The Inspector showed Benson the gun and asked if it was his. Benson said it was not. Inspector Hawkins was not in the least happy about the answers. Back in his office some more clues were starting to fall into place. Several people he had questioned at the office said that Benson was in the habit of carrying a small pistol in his pocket because he often carried large sums of rent money. The manufacturer of the bullets had been traced and every single batch of them had been traced and accounted for with one exception.

The Inspector decided to call on Mr Benson at his house, 66 Taylor Road, Kings Heath on 1 September. Benson continued to state that he had no connection with Sarah Astley; but he had seen her once in Kings Heath. That meeting was quite by chance because Sarah had taken the tram to the top of the village in order to visit her company's younger boss in Featherstone Road. The Inspector repeatedly pressed him about the letter that Sarah had wanted Marion Greene to write to his wife, but he kept denying that there was anything at all between Sarah and him. He went on to elaborate about his movements on the night of the 23rd. He had cycled to Gorcott Hill, through Ullenhall and as far as Bidford on Avon. Quite a ride. He added that he had seen another cyclist, a man from Smethwick returning from his holiday in Gloucester and ridden some way alongside him. Perhaps this man could confirm his alibi. The Inspector had no further leads, and told Benson so. The Inspector told him that despite having no evidence, his story was so much at odds with everyone else's that he would have to attend the Inquest and answer the allegations about his behaviour.

Benson should have known when to leave things alone, but he called to see the Inspector the next morning, having consulted his solicitors. He said he had found a postcard that

Howard Benson lived at 66 Taylor Road. John Marks Collection

confirmed the date that he met Sarah in Kings Heath was actually four years ago. The Inspector pointed out that Sarah's young boss had not moved into Featherstone Road until long after this. Benson left the Inspector in some turmoil. The newspaper appeals by the police had still not found anyone to back up Benson's claim to have cycled in the company of a Smethwick man on the fatal night.

The unaccounted batch of bullets was finally identified and located. It had been sold to a garage owner, and stored loosely in a box on the cluttered desk in the office. Anyone could have picked the bullets up while paying for something in the garage's ironmongery shop. The garage was Bristoll's, Alcester Road South, right at the end of Taylor Road, Kings Heath.

The Benson household was not an easy one on the evening of 3 September. Howard did not sleep in his wife's room, but in his son Leslie's room. They talked over the implications of the inspector's visits. Leslie recalled his father saying , 'It worries me more than you think.'

Leslie was woken from a deep sleep at seven the next morning. His mother was banging on the wall asking where his father was. Leslie replied he thought he was in the garden, and Florence went down to the scullery. There she found Howard lying on his side by the cooker, his head inside the gas oven. He was dead. A note on the table ended with the simple words, 'I can't stand it any longer.'

Had the murderer taken the coward's way out? The police searched the house and found a gun case, without a gun in it. There were cartridges in the case of the same calibre as the gun found in Sarah's hand, but they were not the same batch at all. All his neighbours testified that, as far as they knew, Howard and Florence had lived a perfectly normal and happy life together.

Just what had happened on 23 August? Had Sarah been making love to Howard Benson and had a heart attack, Benson then tried to make it look like a suicide in an effort to keep his name out of the papers. Did Benson intend to kill her for the noise and trouble she was making at the office, humiliating and terrifying her into a seizure and shooting her when he thought she was merely unconscious? There was no firm evidence that he was ever there at all, simply some confused sightings of a man about his height and build, who may, or may not have been wearing a trilby. Was Benson's suicide an admission of his guilt or the desperate act of an innocent man facing the destruction of his family, reputation and career? The coroner's jury found that Sarah had been murdered ... but by person or persons unknown.

Whatever their relationship in life, Sarah Astley and Howard Benson shared a secret that they took with them to the grave.

CHAPTER **30**

Epilogue

H opefully, you are still reading this and not floating in the canal having despaired of human nature. It has been a sorry catalogue of greed, carelessness, callousness and sheer stupidity; but when put in the context of other cities, London for instance, Birmingham turns out to have been a remarkably civilised place. Over the forty years covered by this volume there were very few really wicked murders. There were plenty of alcohol fuelled domestic rows that resulted in a separation more complete than divorce. In the world of murders, your most likely killer is probably looking at you across the breakfast table. After all, your spouse is the one person who knows all your faults and has to put up with them.

A century has passed since the events detailed here. Birmingham itself has changed beyond recognition, whole streets have vanished, tens of thousands of dingy slum houses have been cleared away, replaced by new workshops, tower

blocks of flats and broad roads. Nearly ninety per cent of the houses mentioned in these accounts have gone, a somewhat frustrating figure when it comes to photographing the scenes of crime. The one thing that seems to remain constant is human nature. The headlines of today have changed little in their content. Gangs of youths still

Isaac Bradley succeeded Mr Pemberton as City Coroner. In spite of a particularly depressing sort of job he seems to have maintained a cheerful attitude and sense of humour. Birmingham Weekly Mercury

Mr Pemberton became Coroner in 1891 and started a collection of newspaper cuttings relating to his work that has formed the basis of this book. He was an immensely respected member of the community combining a far sighted intellect with great sympathy for those involved in the tragedies he daily encountered. He died of cancer in 1897. Birmingham Daily Mail.

strut around, usually beating each other up, but occasionally catching innocent bystanders in the crossfire. Marital differences still explode with lethal consequences, although the introduction of divorce has eased the problem. Once in a blue moon some twisted maniac erupts into vicious rage, striking out at random. The motives of most murders remain the same.

Luckily the improvements in health care, typified by the growth of Birmingham's hospitals has led to a marked decline in infant mortality. Children are better fed, and better cared for. Illnesses that swept through the city have largely been eradicated. The coroner no longer has the ghastly but regular task of trying to identify some pathetic little corpse dragged from the canal. Older people too have seen an improvement in their conditions. Although not mentioned a great deal in this book, many hundreds of the elderly descended into poverty once they were too frail to work, and ended their lives with poison, or in the canal. Our welfare system may not be perfect, but when viewed with the perspective of a century, it is a remarkable achievement.

There are some new elements to be found in the 20th century. The Pub Bombings introduced a new depth to the levels of evil that our Victorian ancestors could not have conceived. That ruthless and random act of mass murder has been repeated in almost every city of the world now, but no amount of tragic repetition will erase the memories of the afternoon that the city fell silent.

The complex of buildings that made up the hospital along Dudley Road has nearly all gone now. In its day it was one of the best infirmaries in Europe. John Marks Collection

Winson Green Gaol, the last view of freedom for many of the characters. Once public execution was stopped in 1868, the prison flew a black flag when the criminal was hanged. Later this was replaced with a curt notice pinned to the gates. John Marks Collection

There were plenty of happy endings too... The Strand Magazine

The underworld of drugs has created new problems for society. The Victorians had a morbid terror of sinking into a pit of alcoholic depravity, and to a much lesser extent that of opium addiction. Today the alcohol has been replaced with heroin and cocaine, together with their associated evils. Prostitution remains pretty much the same and is still inescapably linked to addiction, whether booze or drugs. Life on the margins of society is still a precarious affair. The foul deeds of the twentieth century need a volume all to themselves.

Sources

City of Birmingham Coroners' Records, Birmingham Central
  Library.
John Marks Postcard Collection.
Contemporary Newspapers:
  Birmingham Gazette
  Birmingham Argus
  Birmingham Mail
  Strand Magazine
  Daily Mercury

Index

Index of Names